Walk Daily with God: A 365-Day Devotional

A Year of Living in God's Presence

Henry Thomas Hamblin

Hamblin Vision Publishing

Copyright

© Copyright 2025 Hamblin Vision Publishing - all rights reserved.

The content contained within this book may not be reproduced, duplicated or transmitted without direct written permission from the author or the publisher.

Under no circumstances will any blame or legal responsibility be held against the publisher, or author, for any damages, reparation, or monetary loss due to the information contained within this book, either directly or indirectly.

Legal Notice:

This book is copyright protected. It is only for personal use. You cannot amend, distribute, sell, use, quote or paraphrase any part, or the content within this book, without the consent of the author or publisher.

Disclaimer Notice:

Please note the information contained within this document is for educational and entertainment purposes only. All effort has been executed to present accurate, up to date, reliable, complete information. No warranties of any kind are declared or implied. Readers acknowledge that the author is not engaged in the rendering of legal, financial, medical or professional advice. The content within this book has been derived from various sources. Please consult a licensed professional before attempting any techniques outlined in this book.

By reading this document, the reader agrees that under no circumstances is the author responsible for any losses, direct or indirect, that are incurred as a result of the use of the information contained within this document, including, but not limited to, errors, omissions, or inaccuracies.

Contents

Concise Biography of Henry Thomas Hamblin	VI
Introduction	XIX
Preface	XXII
1. January	1
2. February	15
3. March	27
4. April	41
5. May	55
6. June	70
7. July	85
8. August	100
9. September	116
10. October	130
11. November	143
12. December	155
Also by Henry Thomas Hamblin	169

Concise Biography of Henry Thomas Hamblin

By John Delafield, Hamblin's Grandson

Who was Henry Thomas Hamblin?

Henry Thomas Hamblin was a spiritual teacher and writer based in Sussex, England, whose message and vision were straightforward and pragmatic. He believed that the spiritual life and the practical, everyday life were inseparable. His teachings centred around the power of thought and the importance of meditation to draw on the inner power, wisdom and love that we all have deep within us. Hamblin referred to this as 'the Secret Place of the Most High' in the days before meditation was widely practised in the West.

Hamblin was colloquially known as HTH, and later 'the Saint of Sussex'. Whilst his teachings leaned towards esoteric Christianity, his philosophy was truly universal, embracing the truths of all faiths. The emphasis of his message is on finding the power of spirituality within us all, in the context of our everyday lives, rather than religion. As a young man, he reacted against the dogma of his strict, religious upbringing, and believed that religion often divided people, while spirituality united people. His teachings came from a place of pure empathy and compassion for humankind.

Henry Thomas Hamblin worked right up to the end of his life in 1958 and left a legacy that continues to this day, its voice as much needed now as it ever was.

A Wayward Child

Henry Thomas Hamblin was born in 1873 in Walworth, South East London, of Kentish parents, and was the second of two sons. His father was very religious, and his grandfather a minister of the Baptist Church. His mother, although of diminutive size, was reportedly 'great of soul' and ruled the family with benevolent autocracy. The family was poor, very poor, like all those living around them in that district of London in the late Victorian era, and, despite their hard work, the only education that could be afforded for Henry was an elementary one. He followed this with a course in technology, which proved to be of inestimable value to a youth who was considered by his parents and teachers to be wayward.

"Unstable as water; thou shall not excel," his mother reproached him regularly. No doubt she intended it to shame her son into a regime of self-improvement, in keeping with child-rearing practices of the time, but it was hardly confidence-inspiring! "Slacker!" was the repeated insult from his elder brother. Wiser, more objective, heads might have paused for long enough to recognise a certain potential in the young boy who, at the age of nine, could attempt the writing of a school newspaper. He had also established himself as something of an elocutionist. Writing and speaking would both prove valuable skills in later life.

His adolescent years gave little indication of an error in the family verdict. 'Henry the wayward' moved from one poorly-paid post to another, idled in between dead-end jobs, succumbed to bouts of ill-health, and, before he had reached the age of eighteen, had displayed more than the usual 'adolescent failings', according to his autobiography, *The Story of My Life*. From a modern perspective, all these Victorian euphemisms point to Hamblin being something of a 'bad lad', an impression added to by his own heavy hints that he had been no stranger to drinking and carousing. He suffered terribly from pangs of regret following his periods of over-indulgence, so that 'Henry the sinner' became 'Henry the saint' – until the next time. His pronounced rebellious streak landed him in hot water more than once. He constantly pushed against the boundaries of the fire-and-brimstone brand of Christianity in which he had been raised, which he felt to be unbearably restrictive. Reading about his struggles with authority as a young man somehow makes the rather aloof spiritual writer he became more accessible and endearing; it's hard not to warm to someone who so openly confesses their own faults and shortcomings, especially in the tightly buttoned-up era in which he lived. He was inspired by books, many of which fired his worldly ambition and prompted his spiritual imagination.

What his parents and educators overlooked was that Hamblin was a young man with huge aspiration, flushed with a youthful zest for life, and inspired by a worthy ambition to rise above the rut of his circumstances. Although he pushed against his father's dogmatic and punitive style of practising religion, at heart, he was deeply religious. A person's early environment, education, and adolescent behaviour can often determine the course of their life. Youthful indulgences of one sort or another are inevitable. Hamblin's studies of the New Testament, which revealed that selfishness and hypocrisy, rather than indulgence, received greater condemnation by Jesus, would have been very much in his consciousness.

A Successful Businessman

There is no doubt that Hamblin had an enquiring mind, and this, coupled with a desire for scientific accuracy, enabled him to achieve success in his later endeavours in business. In this, despite his lack of education, he was bolstered by boundless faith and courage, which, coupled with a shrewd business sense, ensured that he succeeded beyond all expectation. In 1898, having taught himself ophthalmics at night, he qualified as an optician and set up his first successful business as an optician, Theodore Hamblin (now Dolland and Aitchison), frequented by royalty, the rich and the famous.

Hamblin was a natural entrepreneur and a born risk-taker. By this time, he was also a family man. He married Eva Elizabeth in 1902, and they went on to have two sons and a daughter. He enjoyed acquiring several businesses, all with insufficient capital, and relying on credit and goodwill. He took more pleasure in the thrill of the challenge than in the promise of monetary gain. Far from being downcast in the face of numerous setbacks, he thrived on negotiating obstacles which appeared insurmountable. As soon as the business was established and running smoothly, however, rather than being satisfied with financial security and the ability to provide for his family, Hamblin's interest started to wane. He felt a loss of the initial drive and motivation, his physical and mental health began to decline… until the next big idea came along and away he would charge again, all fired up and raring to go.

Throughout all his wild days of youth and high-risk business ventures, Hamblin felt a great tug towards discovering a deeper meaning to life, beyond that of the daily struggle to make ends meet. Propelled by his discontent, he became a driven seeker after truth. In his quest, he met other prominent thinkers of the time and formed lasting friendships.

As his business success grew, so did a gnawing sense of depression. It was as if there was something inside him that had not yet found a voice. Around this time, he discovered the New Thought movement and began to read their publications. Hamblin realised then that none of his worldly success had made him happy. He felt that a move from London to the coast would be beneficial.

Shortly afterwards came the outbreak of the First World War, and Hamblin went off to serve his country, leaving his business in the care of others, almost with a sense of gleeful relief, strange though it sounds. But it was the sudden and unexpected death of his younger son at the age of ten, in 1918, that brought him to rock bottom and he began to question everything.

A Very Practical Mystic

Hamblin was not a genius, and millions of other people have made good in the world with even less promising assets. But it was in the second half of his life, when Hamblin turned away from creating highly successful business enterprises to focus instead on the spiritual realm, that his unique combination of the pragmatic and the profoundly spiritual shone forth. He has sometimes been described as a very practical mystic.

Hamblin began writing in the 1920s. The words seemed to flow from him. He found that writing clarified his thoughts. One of his first books written in this new phase of his career was *Within You Is The Power*, which was to sell over 200,000 copies. Other books soon followed. Hamblin believed that there is a source of abundance which, when contacted, could change a person's entire life. As long as people blamed their external circumstances for any misfortune, they were stuck in the 'victim role'; but if they moved in harmony with their inner source, their life could be full of abundance and harmony.

Soon after this, Hamblin set up a magazine called *The Science of Thought Review*, based on the principles of Applied Right Thinking. He wasn't discouraged by the fact that he had no experience of editing or publishing. His experience had taught him that if the mind worked in harmony with the Divine, then everything you needed flowed towards you. Anyone with any business sense at all knew that to set up a magazine with a first print run of 10,000 copies would be a risky thing to do. But Hamblin was not risk averse, to put it mildly! He wanted to put what he believed into practice. The only magazine of its kind in the 1920s, it soon gained a worldwide readership. Among his friends and contemporaries that were to contribute to the magazine were Joel Goldsmith, Henry Victor Morgan, Graham Ikin, Clare Cameron and Derek Neville, all of them prolific and successful writers. Apart from his international subscribers, Hamblin had close ties to comparative spiritual thinkers in many other countries, especially in the U.S.

Although he had been brought up in a strictly religious family, he hadn't found any of the answers he sought in the Church. He realised that, rather than following any creed or dogma, which didn't work for him anyway, he had to look within himself. He found contact with 'Presence' and realised it held the key to the peace he was seeking. All the time, his search was leading him nearer to discovering the way his thoughts affected his performance and outlook.

During the General Strike of 1926, the Great Depression of 1929-32, and again in years after the end of the Second World

War, many homeless, unemployed wayfarers came to the Hamblin household seeking relief and shelter. Henry and Elizabeth provided them with a simple meal, new boots and clothing, and money for the road. Hamblin was a man who applied his spiritual principles to his everyday life. Practical Mysticism was Hamblin's life's work. He helped people, in practical ways, to become less fearful, happier, and more successful in their lives. To this end, he wrote books like *The Antidote to Worry*. However, later in life he realised that whilst these books genuinely helped people, they were largely concerned with the personality. He then wished to go a step further and become more fully a truly 'practical mystic', so he wrote a spiritual course of 26 lessons, each with a definite theme presented in a systematic way. This was designed to move beyond the constraints of personality so that the soul could breathe the pure air of Spirit. What was needed, he felt, was 'a total surrender of ourselves to the Divine.' The course is available as the book *The Way of the Practical Mystic*.

The Power of Thought

Hamblin was at the forefront of the New Thought movement which was gaining pace in the early 20th century. He discovered that 'new thought' was, in fact, ancient wisdom, based upon the truth that has always existed since before time began. All great souls give voice to that timeless truth in a myriad of different ways. Hamblin urges us to "Think in harmony with the Universal

Mind." In other words, he underlines the fact that truth is and cannot be changed depending upon our mood or our whim.

Hamblin realised that we need not only a positive frame of mind but an applied way of thinking - Right Thinking, as he termed it. What did he mean by that? Essentially, he defines Right Thinking as:

- Thinking from the Divine standpoint.

- Controlling the thoughts so they do not go off on negative tangents away from the Divine Truth, which is always positive.

- Replacing negative thoughts with positive thoughts.

- Living in the consciousness that all is well; and as an adjunct to this, remembering that perfection exists as a reality now, and to think in the consciousness of that knowledge.

- Meditation or prayer is the highest form of Right Thinking.

- Ultimately, however, the aim is to get beyond thought, 'to enter ultimate truth'.

He said, "When we cease thinking, we glide out on the ocean of God's Peace. Thought brings us to the foot of the mountain after which we have to proceed by intuition."

Health, Wealth and Happiness. Isn't this something we all want, either for ourselves or for those dear to us? And yet, how many of us are struggling to reach or hold such a goal for a sustained period of time?'

Hamblin's teachings explain how we can achieve all of these things, not by hard work and striving but by a simple change of thought. *Within You is the Power* is one of his simple but profound statements, and the title of one of his books.

Hamblin was a prolific author and had many thousands of followers studying and benefiting from his teachings and courses until his death in 1958. The simple principles contained in those teachings are as relevant today as they were when he was alive, and can still help us to achieve health, prosperity and happiness if we apply them conscientiously.

He died in 1958 in Chichester Hospital. The Hamblin Trust exists to this day to propagate the legacy of his work.

The Relevance of his Teachings Today

Hamblin was, essentially, a Christian mystic, yet his ideas about the simplicity and clarity of presence seem incredibly contemporary. He believed that the source of all wisdom is within us and all around us, and that this is the fundamental reality; there is no separation, and we are all one. His message and advice to all who read his work is that it is for everyone and is in harmony with the aspiration of all good people throughout time. Hamblin believed that there can be no finite creed of an infinite faith. Moreover, he suggests that, when creeds appear, true faith can be constrained.

He cautioned that if you seek God in prayer, the corollary is that you must have faith in Him. He often stressed that no prayer goes unanswered, and, although you may not get the answer requested, your prayer will be answered in some form. God is around us and within us, and this is the fundamental reality. He made it clear that, although human organisations come and go, God's laws are eternal, and that God is the quintessence of love, wisdom, and harmony. He expresses the clear view that "Blessed are they who believe and yet have not seen". The knowledge that God is born within us is fundamental to our understanding, and only by the loss of self can God be found. At the point a person surrenders his or her 'self' to God, it is then that a re-birth takes place and one's real life in God begins.

Some may question this view and ask: "What is this but the core teachings of the many brands of Christianity?" In response, Hamblin's view was that modern Christianity is a heterogeneous compound of the teachings of Jesus interwoven with historic pagan-based doubts and fears, litanies, supplications and more, all of which are closely guarded by a priestly hierarchy. These were strong views, and Hamblin does not disparage those who found them uncomfortable, as he says that churches are necessary and helpful for those who are succoured by them. Hamblin had a lifelong rebellious streak where authority was concerned, and this included the strictures of the Church. Hamblin would sometimes say that the Truth of the message of Jesus was so often wrapped up in dogma and creed that its purity and simplicity were obscured.

In his teaching, he states that first comes purity of intention, reminding his readers that one cannot serve God and Mammon. Either you trust God completely or you hedge your bets by having worldly alliances and a healthy bank balance. He maintains that trying to achieve both will impair spiritual development. Secondly, an individual's dedication to following God's path will require great patience, perseverance, faith and courage; but in following this path, the individual will develop forbearance and good will. He adds that other life experiences will follow naturally and lead to a developing compassion, which will enable the individual to radiate the love of God.

Where should we place Hamblin in the long line of mystics, seekers and finders? Perhaps it is rather impertinent to pose the question some 65 years after his death, but it is surely relevant to consider this point as, by any measure, he was an extraordinary person.

Remember that he was born into a life of poverty and obscurity but, despite a very limited education, by superhuman efforts of his imagination, he rose to wealth and secured an esteemed position in life, while all the time being aware of another "self" within him, a spiritual self. Dramatically, in the middle part of his life, he surrendered his material successes to follow his wider calling as a disciple of God. In this later life, he did not subscribe to any specific creed or form of religion. He was no haloed saint in the traditional sense, but he would have said, "What I have done, or rather what has been done through me, can be done by any person in the world according to their gifts and personal faith".

The essence of this teaching is that the latent power of God lies within everyone.

John Delafield is the grandson of Henry Thomas Hamblin and a retired RAF pilot. The majority of his childhood was spent living with his grandparents, Henry Thomas and Elizabeth Eva Hamblin.

Introduction

BY CLARE CAMERON, FORMER EDITOR
OF THE SCIENCE OF THOUGHT REVIEW,
MYSTIC AND POET

The popular *Book of Daily Readings*, compiled by A. Andrews from the writings of the late Henry Thomas Hamblin, founder of *The Science of Thought Review* and author of many books on the interior life of the Spirit, was first published in 1937 and has passed through several editions since. Based on *Right Thinking*, it has served as an instructive, positive, and comforting bedside book for countless readers, as well as a companion for every day.

This new anthology has been compiled by the present editor from the articles which appeared month by month in *The Science of Thought Review* in the following years, until our founder was withdrawn from this long and selfless service at the age of 85 in 1958. We feel there is a need now for this second volume.

The reflections that he was inspired to share with us are for all time, since his life's purpose was to awaken seeking souls to the awareness of the ever-present Divine Reality, which is able to meet every need on every level. He taught us how we might become attuned to it—not by retiring from life's battleground, but by "agreeing with the adversary" in every experience. He said often, even as he was the embodiment of it, that "Love is the key to every situation in life."

To him, as to the mystics of all ages and creeds, the world of the temporal order is one of appearance only. Suffering in all its forms comes from identification with it. Nevertheless, it is undergirded and pervaded by the harmony, order, and beauty of the Divine Archetype, for God is immanent in his creation as well as transcendent. By right attitudes to life, we are enabled to rediscover and play our destined part in God's purpose for humankind. We are all prodigal sons, yet sons and daughters of the Most High.

Before he gave up his worldly career to devote himself entirely to becoming a channel for the Holy Spirit to help others—and the number of lives that have been transformed as a result of his teaching we shall never know—Henry Thomas Hamblin had been a successful businessman and was familiar with all the practical aspects of life. Following an unhappy and lonely childhood, he had received and courageously met more than the average share of ill fortune, tribulation, and sorrow. He was not widely read and referred to himself as a simple man of scant learning. He found his own way to the Truth through prayer, meditation, Bible study, trial and error, and devoted application at every step, and therefore afterwards could write with spiritual authority. He was always very close to his Master, Jesus the Christ.

Here, then, is a selection only. Yet the sensitive reader will discern a prevailing atmosphere of sweetness and light, and sturdy spiritual common sense sufficient for every day, from the pen of one who was—and remains for many of us—a humble English saint in a well-worn suit, known through his writings all over the world, yet comparatively unknown in the corner of English countryside which was his home and where his work is still carried on.

Clare Cameron

Note: We read in greater detail of the way he travelled in his autobiography *The Story of My Life* and its sequel *My Search for Truth*, while his actual teaching as presented in his other books is available from The Hamblin Vision. [1]

---

1. Both books are available from **The Hamblin Vision** website: www.thehamblinvision.org.uk An updated biography is written by Hamblin's grandson John Delafield entitled: "*The Remarkable Life of Henry Thomas Hamblin: Mystic and Successful Businessman*"

Preface

by Henry Thomas Hamblin

Wherever we may go, and whatever we may do, and in whatsoever circumstances we may find ourselves, God is there, His power upholding us, His wisdom guiding us, and His love overshadowing us. It is round about us like an atmosphere.

H.T.H.

CHAPTER ONE

January

January 1

At the dawn of a new year, let us give thanks to God for the way He has led us, for the way He has preserved us, and for the way He has upheld us. How wonderfully we have been blessed! How miraculously we have been preserved from evil. In spite of everything, we have been brought through to this present time.

We have been conscious of divine blessing resting upon us, of the divine presence round about us, of the divine love sustaining us.

Therefore, let us acknowledge that the Lord God omnipotent reigns: that God controls every circumstance of our life: that what God has done, God can do.

January 2

Some people think: "How can I know that God is with me, or His Spirit indwelling me?" The answer to that question is that the very fact that they are seeking something higher than themselves, and are dissatisfied with their present state, and are aggrieved when they fall short – this proves that God is working in them; because of themselves, they could have no desire for higher and better things.

January 3

Evil cannot touch God or even enter His consciousness. Therefore, the true self, being the likeness of God, cannot be affected either. When we say: "Good only can come to me" we mean that this is true of the real spiritual being, who is our real inward self, that which is forever held in the mind of God in unalterable perfection.

Of course, this is useless as a mere intellectual belief, for that can avail nothing. What is needed is an inward realisation. When we realise in our soul that God is good, and God is love, and that He wants to bless us even more than we desire to be blessed, it is like a new birth. We feel set free from great limitations. We feel like a wild bird would feel if, after being confined in a cage, it was set free.

January 4

The slender thread which connects us with reality may come to us in the form of a text, or verse from a hymn learned in childhood, or in a modern statement of truth. When it comes, no matter what form it may be, we recognise it as a message from high heaven itself, the plane of reality and ultimate truth. All that we have to do is to lay hold of it. By so doing, we exercise faith; we put truth into practice; we set forces into motion that work for our highest good.

January 5

Instead of trying to understand everything with our tiny, limited mind, we should trust God with that which is beyond our finite intellect. The way to know God is to trust Him. If we do this, then we learn through experience and direct knowing that which is quite beyond the intellect. We know the deep things of God not through the intellect, but in spite of it.

January 6

Love is always the key, for love draws together in harmony and order, while hate makes everything fly apart, in ever-increasing disharmony and disorder. Love preserves, while hate destroys. Every time that we hate, we begin to destroy ourselves; but every time we exercise Love, we set in motion the healing and restoring power which preserves our life, produces a divine adjustment in our affairs, and brings harmony and order into other lives and, ultimately, the whole world. Indeed, I would go farther and say that setting love in action brings harmony, not only to the visible world, but also to those invisible realms which need such help as we can give; and also to the lower forms of life, both visible and invisible.

January 7

Divine love desires that all may be made happy from their inmost being. This is the great truth which takes a lifetime to learn. Our human reason refutes it. Faith takes a leap in the dark and accepts it, but faith is challenged again and again. If God's love is accepted simply and without questioning, faith will be justified at last.

It is a primary duty to cultivate joy. Wherever we go, we must take our inward joy with us.

January 8

The awakened one is homeless, and yet he is not alone. He is homeless because he has been cut adrift from attachment to material things, so that he realises with St. Paul that "for here we have no abiding city, but we seek one to come".

But while, as far as this world is concerned, we are homeless, yet we are not alone. For the more we become separated from the world, the nearer we are drawn to God. The more we become dissatisfied with the transient things of this life, the more satisfied we become in God. The less we depend on other people, the more completely we become aware of the sustaining presence of God.

January 9

It is when we trust God, even to the extent of losing all, even our soul, that we find God, really and truly. We cannot find God through reading a book, but only through experiment and experience. If we put the little fragment of truth which we possess into practise, then greater understanding comes to us. In the same way, if we trust God fully, then we find God truly.

January 10

At a time of crisis, let us remember that God controls every circumstance of our life, and that circumstances and events do not control us, although they appear to do so. Directly a thought of fear, confusion, apprehension, hopelessness or anxiety comes into our own minds, let us dismiss it by declaring that God (creator and ruler of the whole universe) controls every circumstance of our life. It is very simple, but very effective. We do not need to be learned, clever, or even wise; all that we have to do is to declare this simple truth, that God controls every circumstance of our life, including this present experience.

January 11

If we always realised that God controls everything, then things would not get out of control, as in the case in the world at the present time. Things "get out of hand" because we do not acknowledge God in all our ways. We are promised that if we acknowledge God in all our ways, then He will direct our paths...and then we are always in our right place at the right time.

> I do not ask that God's will should be done in order that my life may be made easier for me, but rather that all that hinders the life of God in me may be dissolved away.

January 12

Divine order can manifest only if we abandon ourselves to the divine will to do with us as it wills, for it itself is the divine order. Divine order cannot possibly reign in our life and affairs if we do not allow it to do so, for it will not force itself on anyone.

January 13

When we enter into a state of realisation, we know what the breathing of the Spirit is, for, without any trying on our part, we find that our breathing has become as deep as the universe. Not only has it become deep, indescribably so, but also it has become conformed to an inward rhythm, so that we breathe in correspondence with the Spirit, and with the whole universe.

January 14

We are ministered unto in a thousand different ways. From every direction, love ministers to us through a thousand different channels. It makes us feel very humble and unworthy. It makes us feel how much we owe, and how deeply indebted we are to those who give themselves for us. The least we can do is render all the service we can in return, to live less selfishly, and to pour out all that we have and are in love to the whole.

This is what breaks down the hard shell of our self-centredness and selfishness, the thought that so much is being done for us, while we give so little in return.

January 15

If we resent and rebel against the experiences of life, then life becomes increasingly difficult and painful. The more we try to resist life's experiences, the more complicated our life becomes, because by our resistance, we force ourselves away from the middle of the stream of life. Life is like a stream or river along which we are carried, whether we like it or not. So long as we keep to the middle, all goes well; but if we forsake the middle and drift off to the sides, then we become caught up in all sorts of entanglements. If we accept life's experiences and cooperate with them, we are kept in the middle of the stream of life and maintained in a state of blessedness.

January 16

If people only realised what takes place when they pray, they would do more of it. When we pray, we become attached to all the powers of light and order. We become lifted up above the powers of darkness and disorder and raised into heavenly places. Thus, it becomes possible for light and power, joy and peace, order and perfection, to flow through us to the world.

January 17

A common question is: "Why is it, now that I'm trying to live a life of faith, I am being so severely tested?". The answer is, of course, that we can never learn really to know God and enter into His freedom without experiencing what Whittier describes in his poem:

> Nothing before, nothing behind:
> The steps of faith
> Fall on the seeming void, and find
> The rock beneath.

January 18

As you lean back upon the everlasting arms, you will be upheld, sustained and supported; all will be well with you, and you will be brought victoriously through this experience, and also through all life's experiences, and upheld in all the great crises of life.

Love does not want you to mourn or grieve. Love wants to fill your life and heal your heart. Love wants to be all to you, and to be more, far more to you than even that which you may have lost.

Love wants to raise you to higher and better things. Love wants to give you the hidden peace and satisfy all the longings of your soul.

January 19

How much can I love? And how best can I serve? These are the things which give joy and a deep satisfaction in God. But we do not practise them for reward, but only for the sake of doing them. When a lover offers a gift to their beloved, he wants no return, but to give for love's sake alone. It is the same with giving our love to the world. Love compels us. We love the world so much that we must pour out our soul upon all humankind, and give all that is within us, both to God and man.

January 20

What does a child do when it is overtired? It rests in its mother's arms. In the same way, if we are spent and cannot even pray, then we should simply rest in the love of God, relax, let go, and lean back on the everlasting arms. When we cannot pray, or read our spiritual books, it is a sure sign that the Spirit does not want us to attempt any of these things. It is a sign that the Spirit wants us to rest and recuperate.

January 21

If we do that which the indwelling Lord wants us to do, then we become filled with peace and heavenly joy. If, however, we do that which is against the Spirit's will, then we become strained, uneasy, apprehensive and unhappy.

Blessed is the one who always follows the inner guidance of the indwelling spirit of Jesus Christ, for he is led in paths of order, harmony and peace.

It does not matter what name we give to the indwelling one, the essential thing is that we should realise and acknowledge his presence or spirit within us, and walk in union with him.

January 22

Divine care, in its deeper sense, is not the result of praying to God to protect us, so much as our becoming adjusted to the divine order and to life in general. First of all, we become enlightened through staying our mind upon God in prayer and contemplation (or inward communion with God) so that we know truth by direct soul cognition. Thus, we become adjusted towards God. As a result of this, we are able to project our love outwards to all, like beams of light from a lighthouse. Thus do we become completely adjusted both to God and humanity; to the above and below; to the inner and outer; to the unseen and to the seen.

January 23

Underneath the surface of life there is a delightful unity and harmony. In order to find it and realise our oneness with it, our heart has to be filled with love to all creation, and also, we must put aside all care, disentangling ourselves from the things which fret and grieve. Then perhaps, at some unexpected moment, it is as though a door in our soul opens, and for a brief space we become conscious of the great unity and oneness with the interior order and harmony flowing through everything. We find ourselves at one with the whole universe, and in a state of sweet, ineffable joy, such as cannot be described.

January 24

It makes a great difference to our health if we practise raising our thoughts to higher things. This in itself may be insufficient to heal us, but it makes it possible for a power greater than ourselves to heal us. Also, if we try to bring our mind into harmony and correspondence with the divine order, we are helped by the spirit to do so. We cannot deliver ourselves, but if we do our best to rise mentally above our ordinary limited thought-life, then we are given power by the spirit to do so. We have to do our part, after which the divine action takes place.

January 25

Ideas come from the invisible and clothe themselves with suitable atoms which also come out of the invisible. Invisible substances whipped into a vortex, and lo, a world is born! There is nothing fixed, everything is fluidic. Atoms come from the invisible and pass back into the invisible. Archetypal ideas remain, but the atoms which clothe these ideas come and go. Manifestations may be fleeting, but the one life remains.

January 26

Every experience that comes to a child of God is designed to remove part of the wrappings which cover up the inward light. If these experiences are accepted, and co-operated with, then gradually the light grows in intensity and splendour as the wrappings are removed. First, there is the faint dawn, next the sunrise, after which comes the splendour of the noonday; corresponding to first the blade, then the ear, after that the full corn in the ear.

January 27

Love pours its blessings upon us with ever-increasing measure. And this is the more overwhelming when we remember that we have no true love of our own, but that the love which makes us pour out our soul in benediction, compassion and mercy upon all humankind, and upon all creation, is not of ourselves, but is the love of God which has entered our heart and is changing us into its own likeness.

January 28

People often write saying that they have prayed most earnestly to God for a long time about a certain thing, but that nothing has happened. Such prayers, probably, were of such a kind as to deepen the sense of lack and limitation instead of removing it. They may have prayed about their trouble instead of seeking to see the thing as it is in God: they may have prayed about the thing as it is according to appearances, instead of as it is eternally in the mind of God, in infinite perfection.

January 29

Everyone who essays to live a life of faith may pass through a barren period or experience a time of adversity, for it is only by testing and trials that faith can be increased. If, however, our heart is right with God, we can bear this with equanimity, for we know that if we are patient, and if, taking hold of God's hand with confidence and trust, we step out with him into the unknown, then we shall be brought victoriously through all life's experiences.

January 30

Attainment does not drop into our lap in response to wishful thinking, or even wishful praying. It has to be won in the same way that every other prize must be won. We cannot stay our mind upon God simply by daydreaming and wishing. No, we have to wait upon God daily, and continually to keep in living contact with our divine source.

January 31

We can look within to the inmost recesses of our being and hear the indwelling Lord speak to us in *soundless* tones:

> Come unto me and find in me the light of life.
> Come unto me, the light which lights all who come into the world.
> I am your indwelling Lord.
> You have ignored me all your life; you have searched for truth everywhere, but you have not found it;
> you have looked for me outside of yourself while all the time I have been patiently waiting for you to discover me deep within your own being.
> You have searched the scriptures, trying to find in them eternal life, but only in me can you find what you seek,
> for to know me in itself, is eternal life.

Chapter Two

February

February 1

Every man is the inlet, and may become the outlet, of all there is in God.

                                    Ralph Waldo Emerson

If we try to be the outlet and will give what we have, that is, if we empty ourselves in giving, then we shall become the inlet. Even more, we shall become a universal chalice.

February 2

If we place truth before those who are not yet ready for it, they resent it, reject it, or fail to understand it. Later on, they may accept it gladly, and may seek it here, there and everywhere. But they themselves have not brought about the change. It is the work of the indwelling spirit.

After hearts have been changed by the divine spirit of truth it is possible to help people by stressing the necessity of changing the thoughts and also showing them how to do so.

February 3

At the centre all is stillness. It is the source of all order and harmony. Just as a wobbling wheel becomes apparently motionless when it has been correctly centred, so also do we find peace through our whole personality directly we become centred in God. Jesus asked that those for whom He prayed might be in Him and He in them, thus forming a perfect union and oneness. We experience this when we find ourselves filled with God's inward peace, and at the same time feel that we're being carried along on a river of God's peace.

February 4

We go forward in stages, and we have to struggle and fight at first, but finally we come to the stage in which we can let go and allow God to bring about a divine adjustment. So that, instead of trying to do everything ourselves, we allow the spirit to work through us without effort or strain. In point of fact, this is the very thing we strive for. We struggle in order to reach that state of consciousness which is above all struggle.

February 5

Faith enables us, in creative thought, to get beyond our limitations, to push back the boundaries of the human mind, so that what is termed the impossible can become possible. There is nothing impossible with God. There is nothing impossible with the invisible mind-stuff in which we are immersed. What we have to do is to form the image in mind-stuff of a richer, fuller and more abundant life, which is really a faint glimpse of that which is really true, and which is God's idea of perfection concerning us.

February 6

Love is invincible if we apply it as a dynamic power. If we do not apply it in this way, it remains potential or static. The power is there, but it is not put into action. Consequently, in spite of it being [potentially] present, yet as far as practical results are concerned, it might just not be there at all.
Immediately, however, we begin to use love as a dynamic force, directing it like a searchlight beam, we've put in motion a power that is invincible, because love is omnipotence in motion.

February 7

The essential thing for us to do is to know how to walk according to divine counsels and in accordance with the divine idea and pattern of perfection. This we can discover through looking within to the indwelling spirit of truth and wisdom, whose voiceless counsel is always ready to indicate the right path for us to take. When we propose to take a certain course of action which is in harmony with the divine plan and pattern of perfect order and blessedness, we become filled with heavenly joy and peace. But should we decide to take the wrong road, we become filled with unrest.

February 8

Those who seek divine healing must learn to relax and let go, so that the Lord who is their true life may restore them. Self-effort tends to prevent the mysterious change which takes place when we are divinely healed. We have to allow the Lord [the one perfect life] to heal us by leaving off personal straining and striving to heal ourselves. Self-effort may have been so successful in the past that it may seem difficult, if not impossible, to surrender ourselves to a greater and higher power now.

February 9

When, instead of living at the circumference, we learn to abide at the centre and source of all things, we find the rock under our feet, so that our life becomes stable and secure.

The secret of all power and true success is to abide at the centre. There we become stabilised and one with the eternal. There we can "watch the world go by, to know no gain or loss". There we realise that we do not belong to the passing show, but that we are one with the unchanging reality.

February 10

Although we may find ourselves in the most upsetting conditions, amid scenes of disorder and anxiety, yet God is not far away. He has not removed his presence. Actually, his presence is with us as much as ever it has been in the past. What has happened is that we have allowed ourselves to get outside of it - we have got into a wrong consciousness.

February 11

Continually harping on dying to self is a mistake, for - at least it so seems to the writer - it focuses the attention not on Christ but on ourselves and our shortcomings. Consequently, there is a perpetual conflict going on which leads to misery and also prevents progress. It also produces a form of religious ego-centricism which is harmful and stultifying. This means that we think too much about ourselves, and this holds us back. ...

The remedy is simple and effective. We need to become perfectly quiet by stilling the agitated surface mind ... By calling on the name of the Lord Jesus, the wind and waves of our stormy mind can be hushed and quietened so that there comes a great calm and peace. Then we can contemplate quietly and restfully our highest conception of the Christ - his purity, his patience, his love, his harmony, his peace and joy.

February 12

When the higher consciousness is opened up, we are, as it were, in God's holy mountain. We are raised up above the plane on which evil operates and has limited sway. Therefore, we are assured: "They shall not hurt, nor destroy in all my holy mountain, saith the Lord". They, the disturbers of our peace; they, the fears which assail us, shall have no power over us, so long as we are maintained on the higher consciousness.

But we must not allow our thoughts to go back to the old order of thinking. We must keep our mind in the consciousness that interiorly we are one with the eternal.

February 13

There are many people who keep on affirming, "I and my Father are one", in the hope of someday realising divine union. But Jesus made his statement after He had realised his oneness and unity with the Father. He did not go about repeating the statement as an affirmation which, by constant repetition, might one day be found true. No, He spent hours, even whole nights, in communion with the Father.

February 14

Laying up treasure means raising our consciousness to the highest point of union. Every time that we do this and contemplate the ineffable, we lay up treasure in heaven. That simply means that it becomes increasingly less difficult for us to look into eternity, so that it becomes almost as easy as looking out of the window. This leads to a permanent state of heavenly mindedness, or God-consciousness, and this is what constitutes treasure in heaven.

February 15

Before we can pass into the secret place, we have to exfoliate all our knowledge, all our love of self and attachment to worldly things, until at last, having laid aside everything, we come to nothing. And when we come to nothing, we discover that we have found everything. It is then that the action of God can take place.

February 16

Some remarkable things are taking place in the world at the present time, and those who are labouring for righteousness may take heart in the fact that the real world carries on in infinite order and perfection. Those who have put God out of their lives and who think they can do just what they please, in defiance of divine law, may meet with a great shock. Righteousness shall prevail. Evil and lawlessness always defeat themselves.

February 17

Every grief and sorrow patiently borne, every trouble faithfully met, every problem solved through prayer and waiting upon God, every task lovingly performed, all these help to build up and add to the inner celestial body. The Christ in us increases, while the self decreases, until at last we reach the measure of the stature of the fullness of Christ.

February 18

Students are apt to think that their teachers or leaders are immune from problems. They think that those who possess [or claim to possess] such a wonderful understanding of truth can never meet with any problems at all. As a matter of fact, the only difference between teacher and student is that the former has greater problems and more searching experiences than the latter. But, of course, by tackling them at once, the teacher is raised above them, so that the effect is that problems, difficulties and so-called frustrations raise them to higher things, and make great attainment possible.

February 19

I take my stand in truth. I can do nothing more than this. Of myself, I can do nothing, but truth is omnipotent and has nothing to oppose it; therefore, it is able to work its perfect way and to manifest itself. No error, or evil, or darkness, can stand against it. Truth has no adversary. When we apprehend, recognise and realise truth, we find that all that is not truth has disappeared; that truth stands alone, because there is nothing, really, but truth.

February 20

God is able to supply our need out of his riches in glory. This means out of the inexhaustible substance which is the foundation of all earthly substance. Divine creative mind supplies the ideas, which translated into form, bring into objectivity the things that we need. There may be seeming lack of material things, but God's riches can never fail. Infinite mind can bring to us, through human channels, all that we need.

February 21

The object of prayer is not to get things, or to beg for favours. Neither is it a demand for what are termed demonstrations. Neither should it be an attempt to alter the mind of God, but rather to attune our mind to the mind of God. Its object is not to alter the will of God, which is perfect, but to bring our will into conformity with the will of the highest. It is not to change the all-wise imagination, but to bring our foolish, wayward imagination into a state of oneness with it.

February 22

In this present life, we are able to live consciously on this material plane through our material body. Without it, we should simply be a disembodied spirit. But, through prayer, meditation and contemplation, there is built up within us an everlasting body of light substance. This endures through the aeons and knows no decay, because it is composed of indestructible elements...a house not made with hands, eternal in the heavens.

February 23

Let us consider what a state of divine blessedness is. When we live in a state of blessedness, everything is in its right place at the right time. We live in a state of wholeness and completeness, there being no lack or limitation. Whatever our life may need comes to us, at the right time. We live by faith in God, instead of depending upon material resources. We are protected from a thousand ills and dangers, for there are no such things in the divine order.

February 24

Before we can occupy a higher place, we have to be attuned to it. And this, after all, is the real object of meditation – that we might become attuned to the vibrations of heaven. When we have achieved this, and have become attuned to the atmosphere of heaven, it becomes possible for us to rise in consciousness out of time into eternity.

February 25

It marks a great advance in our spiritual unfoldment when we can see God everywhere, in all people, in all circumstances and in every experience. We are able to make friends with the unwanted experiences of life and agree with our adversary, and go the other mile, because we know that God's hand is in everything and that nothing but good can come to us.

February 26

Our aim should always be to overcome our depression by rising above it. We should try to feel as light-hearted and happy as we would if we were already on top of our trouble and out of darkness. This calls for perseverance and persistence. Instead of being overcome by life's troubles and the blows of adversity we turn them into stepping stones and rise to higher and better things. If we feel rich, we shall never be poor: if we feel well, we shall retain our health: if we feel successful, we shall find ourselves so. Such "feeling" of course is inward and deep down.

February 27

William Blake said that if the doors of our perception were cleansed then we should see things as they are, infinite. What we see and experience is largely a reflection of our thoughts. Those who complain of being low-spirited, dull and liverish, would probably become transformed if they were to receive some good news. Far better would it be if they were to make contact with the heavenly world around them through prayer and meditation.

February 28

It is easy for us to think that the peoples of the world need to be changed, and to forget that it is we who must first be altered. The change of heart and thoughts must first be wrought in us and not in others. It has to take place in our personal life, in our own home, in our street or village – in this very spot, where we are at this moment. We have to build up our own life in this very place, in these very circumstances. We have to learn to forgive now, all the wrongs that have been done to us. It is necessary that we should meet with these difficult experiences that we might learn the art of forgiveness. When we realise this, it becomes easier for us to accept life's experiences and co-operate with them.

CHAPTER THREE

March

March 1

We cannot drag God down to our level; if we are to be lifted up to His peace we must be lifted up to His level. Our vibrations have to be raised, so to speak; we have to be brought into a higher key in order to vibrate at the divine level. We are told to be still and know God.

March 2

Yes, God is able. His strength is made manifest in our weakness, so that "when I am weak, then am I strong". His victory is made manifest in our defeat. His success appears when we have failed utterly. And it is all for us. He loves us with an everlasting love, and with loving kindness does He draw us. All blessings may be ours if we will trust Him, instead of relying upon people, or things, or circumstances.

March 3

This one creative power (God) is capable of creating a million universes, with millions of suns, of galaxies, of nebulae such as cannot be described. Yet Jesus taught us to call God "our Father". Not an infinite power beyond our reach, but an intimate being whom we could address as our Father, and who was instantly and at all times available. Consequently, we are able to tap infinite resources at any time through "our Father".

March 4

Some may ask: "How can loving our enemies and doing good to those that hate us, how can that prevent war? How can that save the world from itself?" The answer is that we are all members of one another, and we are all part of one complete whole. Consequently, what we do individually affects everyone else. If we love and forgive, and if we pray for our enemies, then everyone is blest, including ourselves. We set in motion currents of healing and blessing which flow to all people. The future of humankind lies not in the hands of the great and mighty, but rather in the hands of the lowly and humble who seek God's inward peace in prayer.

March 5

It does not matter what our problem may be, God is the sole remedy. Therefore, we do not pray about our trouble, neither do we ask that it be removed, we simply move right into the midst of it and pronounce the word GOD. "God is in the midst of her, she shall not be removed". [Psalm 46.5]. We put our whole trust in God and are prepared to accept His way rather than our own. This involves acceptance. We can overcome a difficulty only by first accepting it. Consequently, we do not run away from trouble, for to do so would but increase its power over us. Neither do we fight or resist it. We simply bring the divine order into it, by uttering the word GOD.

March 6

Many people say that they cannot pray: they do not know what to say. They think they must be eloquent, and they must possess a gift for prayer. But it is not so. If they were to say the word GOD they would be helped; while if they were to repeat the name in the face of all their fears, doubts, troubles and impending disasters, they would enter into a measure of "the peace which passes all understanding".

March 7

The invisible forces of the spirit are far more potent than those of the human mind and will. The activities of man based on selfishness and self-interest may threaten the peace of the whole world, and it is impossible to overcome them by employing the worldly methods of force, resistance and destruction, but the powers of the spirit can defeat them. The spiritual power of love is greater than the power of hate. The spiritual person can invoke the infinite powers of the absolute.

March 8

If in winter our tanks, water pipes, etc., are frozen hard, we may find it does more harm than good trying to free them by using hammer and chisel; yet, if we apply heat, the whole trouble passes away almost like magic. It is the same when dealing with hatred and the forces of evil; if we retire into the unseen and realise God's peace, the hatred melts away and violence gives place to peace.

From this we see that the issues between life and death lie not with the strong and mighty, but with those awakened souls who are capable of retiring into the hidden strength, and who can love those who hate them, and who can invoke the power of the supreme.

March 9

The ability to rise into the divine consciousness comes to us as a gift of divine grace. "In a moment, in the twinkling of an eye…we shall be changed". It is nothing that we do, actually. It is something that comes to us when we least expect it. Suddenly, we glide out into a larger consciousness – the spiritual consciousness, which never was born and never can die. Our breathing becomes deep and rhythmic of its own volition, and we know deep down within our soul that our life has infinite extensions beyond time and space.

March 10

Our breathing is of great importance. When we relax and the deep breathing of the hidden life comes upon us, we must be ready to receive it, so that it can take possession of us. Many people do not know how to breathe so deeply that it seems as deep as the universe. This cannot be achieved by strain and effort but only by relaxing and letting go, thereby allowing the life of God to have free course in and through us.

March 11

Praise be, God is able to do for us far more wonderful things than ever we dream of asking or even imagining. God is able. He has the ability. He has established an eternal principle which never alters or fails, and which, if complied with can, and always does and will, accomplish the impossible, and do great things for us, whereof we are glad.

March 12

Some cannot understand why it is that when we run after things they evade us, and that when we stand still, they come to us. The explanation is that when we run after things we adopt a negative attitude and emphasise the fact that we are in a state of need and deficiency. This, of course, tends to increase or perpetuate our trouble or sense of inadequacy. If, however, we cease "the joyless quest of the human mind" and stand in the eternal ways, then we become positive. We realise that we are at the centre [God] and that all the divine forces are hastening to minister to us, while every needed blessing is coming to us just at the right moment. Consequently, instead of rushing about seeking divine blessing, we "stand still and see the salvation of the Lord".

March 13

It is possible to live in both worlds at once, and this takes place every time we pray, meditate and experience God's inward peace. It is also possible to rise in consciousness to heavenly realms and realise our true identity as children of God. Also, as a result, a divine adjustment takes place in our affairs, according to infinite wisdom and infinite love.

March 14

We can all help the world by being forerunners of a new way of life, in which we "live by faith and not by sight", in which also we trust the unseen, instead of relying on the seen, in which also we rely upon the spirit rather than material powers or human intellect.

Those who go the whole way, that is, those who wish to dedicate lives wholly to God and humanity, will work for love's sake and not for reward. They will work as industriously and strenuously as those who work to satisfy their ambitions, but all that they do will be done as an act of service and not for reward to be seen of men and women.

March 15

There is a divine prosperity and an infinite and inexhaustible abundance, which is always present with us, ready to be poured out, according to our trust and faith. When we give, we must not think that we are giving away our substance, but that we are drawing upon God's invisible and infinite resources. It is like the widow's cruse of oil. Directly we empty our coffers in love and service, and as an exercise of faith, they become replenished, so that the more we give out, the more we receive. It is the operation of divine law.

March 16

Every thought of fear and resentment can be countered by declaring that "the Lord God Omnipotent reigns". The fate of the world does not rest with dictators or other heads of nations, but we are all in the hands of God. We are content to go God's way; we are content to do God's will: we desire only that the will of God should be done, both in our own lives and in the lives of others.

March 17

There is a great paradox – we try to achieve the impossible and fail, yet it is in this failure that our reason becomes transcended. When our knowledge fails, awareness begins, and we experience the truth of St. Paul's words that spiritual things can be spiritually discerned, whereas they are quite beyond the human mind. We have to fail before we can succeed: we have to go down before we can be raised up.

March 18

People act destructively, and harm themselves and the community more from ignorance than from evil desire. For instance, if robbers suddenly had revealed to them the secret of divine supply, they would cease to be robbers; for there would be no advantage gained by robbing others. Again, if it were generally known that we receive back from life exactly what we give, nobody would harm another, because they would know that if they were to do so, they would be harming themselves.

Alas, that the teaching of Jesus has never been followed, for if it had, the world by now would have become a paradise of delight.

March 19

When we are in the true silence, the Holy Spirit takes control, and we become moved right to the very core of our being. We feel shaken, as though we had passed through a great soul experience, such as is beyond any human understanding. It is then that the world is blessed. Waves of spiritual power sweep outwards through space in all directions, to the north, to the south, the east and the west. Then it is that those who are ready for it receive a blessing. They receive as much enlightenment as they are ready for.

March 20

If people generally realised the invisible power of thought, they would cultivate different thought habits. If they knew that thoughts of hatred and ill will produced evil results thousands of miles away; and if they knew that they had a boomerang effect they would surely try to cultivate thoughts of love, kindness and goodwill. What we are experiencing today in our lives is the result of past thinking. Every evil or negative thought brings back to us some form of suffering, while every good and generous thought comes back to us in the form of blessing and harmony.

March 21

We can meet an unwelcome experience in three wrong ways: (1) we can run away from it or try to shirk it; or (2) we can fight and resist it; or (3) we can try to think that it does not exist, by denying its existence and calling it illusion. The right way to meet it, of course, is to face up to it, accept it, and deal with it in love. We cannot make a thing any less real by denying it; also, if we run away from an experience, it follows us, no matter where we may go, and repeats itself in an aggravated form. If we fight it, we may soon find ourselves in a hornet's nest of quarrels.

If, however, we accept the experience and deal with it in love, it becomes an entrance to a new life of overcoming and high achievement.

March 22

Experience has taught me that it is not only necessary to acknowledge and recognise the presence of God, but it is also just as necessary to declare that God's presence is love. Love possesses a miraculous power and potency; and by "Love" I mean God's love, or God as love, acknowledged and declared by us in face of disorder and difficulty. Actually, I cannot describe love, for it is beyond any description. It heals, adjusts, and makes all things new. That is all I can say.

All I know is that it is beyond all our human ideas of love. A person who has experienced it can never describe it, but life for them can never be the same again.

March 23

Some middle-aged and elderly people are appalled when they look back on their past life, with its lost opportunities and the many grievous mistakes made, involving other lives and bringing suffering to others. They feel that such complications can never be healed and that their own suffering or loneliness at the present time is merely the fruitage of their past errors, and therefore it is too late for any remedy to be possible.

But if they will acknowledge their shortcomings and will recognise God in this long drawn-out experience, that He is at the centre and heart of it, and that He is love, they will not only find rest for their soul, but they will also find that God, because He is love, is able, and does heal and restore and overrule everything for good. So that in a most wonderful way, quite beyond our understanding, everyone who has been involved is blessed and benefited.

March 24

No matter what our age and circumstances may be, to go forward in faith will integrate us and our life; while hanging back and trying to avoid life's challenges and duties will just as surely disintegrate us and our life. A state of integration not only repels evil happenings; it also attracts all manner of good. In addition, a person who is integrated is able to help others; while a disintegrated person cannot do so.

March 25

At times in our life, when experiencing glimpses of cosmic consciousness, we become aware of beauty beyond description and a light which suffuses all. Everything is shot through with glory. For a few seconds we realise that perfection is the reality, and that it is always with us, standing behind the world of imperfection (or far country) into which we have wandered.

We then realise that what is needed is a change of consciousness on our part. We have not to change the world so much as to become changed ourselves. Our flashes of cosmic consciousness reveal to us that if our everyday consciousness were changed so that we were always in that state, then either the world would be changed or healed, or we would find that it did not require either changing or healing.

March 26

Life is the great initiator. It is through the experiences of life that we are brought back to God. We need no societies, no initiation rites, for each experience in life is an initiation in itself, which, if met fairly and cooperated with, advances us in the process which changes us into correspondence with the Divine likeness.

March 27

In order to use truth, we need to exercise faith. It requires faith on our part to declare truth (which is the thing as God sees it, and not as it appears to mortal sense) in the face of everything that appears to be the exact contrary. It requires faith on our part to fling truth boldly in the face of an evil happening which is developing in such a way as to fill us with fear and foreboding. What is needed then is to cleanse the mind completely of fear, and this can be done by filling it with truth. Fighting against our fears will do no good. They can only be driven out through an influx of truth. We can say:

There is nothing in all the universe which can make me afraid, for I am upheld by all the power of the living God (or Ever-Living One).

We can say this with confidence, because it is absolutely true; that is, it is truth as it is in God, for each one of us is upheld, sustained and supported by the Divine Spirit, all through life.

March 28

Let us commit then our way unto the Lord, who is the author of the light and the glory. When Jesus came, He opened a door into the Light Realms through which their glory and radiance could shine into this darkened world. He was the first-born among many siblings who were to become light bearers and door-openers also.

Let us then commit our way unto the Lord, so that the light, the glory, and the radiance of the Light Realms may shine into the shadowed world.

March 29

When someone prays, if they pray earnestly enough and long enough, their mind gradually becomes attuned to the mind of God, so that finally it works in harmony and correspondence with it, thus producing order in place of disorder. If results are delayed, it is not because God does not hear, for such is a pagan idea; neither is it because God is unwilling to bless; but is simply due to the fact that our mind is so unlike God's mind it takes necessarily a long time to bring it into tune and correspondence.

March 30

We see those for whom we want to pray with their faces turned towards the light, marching towards the hills of God. We see them sinless, stainless, made whole by Thee, filled with joy and peace, purity and truth, and rejoicing in the joy of Thy salvation. We thank Thee because they are free and unafraid and crowned with the light and glory of Heaven. We see them going from strength to strength and from victory to victory, surrounded by Thy glory and radiance. We see them filled with the Christ-love and pouring it out upon all humankind.

March 31

A providence of love is making sweet the very springs of our life. This divine providence of love turns everything to good account, sweetens with eternal good every experience, and overrules everything for good, if we will only allow God's will to be done. God's will is the expression of the providence of love. That is why we are taught to pray that God's will should be done on earth, as it is in Heaven.

It would be just as correct to pray: "Let Thy providence of love have free course in my life and affairs."

CHAPTER FOUR

April

April 1

We pray to be healed, not in order to be more comfortable, but in order that we may be more useful. Thus, actually we do not pray for ourselves, but for others, when we pray that a divine adjustment may by the grace of God be brought about in our life, our body and affairs. We can hardly expect God to heal us if we are not determined to use such health and vigour as may be given us in the service to the world, our day and generation.

April 2

It makes a great difference if, instead of looking upon our trouble as trouble merely, we regard it as a discipline and training through which we can attain to a closer union with God. It may be due to our own wrongdoing in the past, but if so, it is a redemptive or remedial experience which contains within itself a great blessing. It may, however, be something which we have taken on voluntarily, and if so, it will also be a redemptive experience, but in this case the effect will be the redemption of the world.

April 3

Finding the midpoint or secret place of the most high is the greatest healing and restoring agent of all, but of course the right attitude of acceptance and cooperation must be established first. If we find the secret place, we reach that point which was [and eternally is] that which God was before humanity's contrary will and false imagination arose [or arises]. We get back to that point which is beyond the pairs of opposites, and which reconciles them and where all duality and conflict disappear.

April 4

If we do not practise the truth which we know, then we lose it. "If any one will do His will, they shall know of the doctrine". It is not doctrine which saves and blesses us but doing the will of God. If we do that, then the understanding of truth will follow. Within ourselves is an inexhaustible fountain or reservoir of truth, which gradually opens up and rises into consciousness to the extent that we put the truth that we know into practise.

April 5

It may not sound very helpful to be told that we can only learn through experience. But by this, we do not necessarily mean suffering. God has provided a better way than that of mere suffering. It is true that we have to accept life's experiences and be ready to endure all things, but if we come into union with Jesus who is the inner fountain or order, the interior harmony, and principle of perfection, then we find that the yoke is easy and the burden light.

We are so apt to struggle and to strive, to want to battle all by ourselves, wearing ourselves out in the process. But Jesus says: "Come unto me, and I will give you rest".

April 6

As far as experience is concerned, if we agree with our adversary, bless the undesired discipline, and then apply love in full measure, we make the path, difficult though it may be, much easier than it would be otherwise. If it is very thorny, then perhaps it may be due to the fact that we're not applying enough love.

April 7

Most people live at the circumference of life, but it is possible to dwell at the centre, in a state of union with that which creates all things. Such do not pray for "things" to come to them, but they express them. As they move forward, all that they need for their work and, incidentally, for their subsistence, manifests before them.

All visible things around us are a manifestation of the invisible, true, inward reality and substance. They spring into being as an expression of the creative power and intelligence which we term God or spirit. When we become at one with this central creative power, i.e. when we become God-conscious through union – then we do not pray for things, but instead we express or manifest them.

April 8

Experience shows that if we look to other people to help us, then as a result, we always find ourselves in a state of lack. ... If however, we refuse to look to other people, but rely instead on the power of God within us, and if, in addition, we try to help other people, and other good works, in an attempt to give rather than to receive, then we find ourselves always in a state of divine supply and plenty, each legitimate need being met without anxiety or calculation or planning.

April 9

One who takes up the faith attitude, trusting in invisible fountains and hidden resources, adopts the most positive attitude possible, so that everything that they need flows towards them instead of away from them.

Through being in a state of union or oneness with the indwelling Almighty Spirit, we express the things needed, or they come tumbling over themselves, so to speak, in their strong desire to manifest in our life and work.

April 10

The object of prayer is not to attempt to alter the mind, will or purpose of God, but rather to conform our mind to the divine mind. Our distress and disharmony are due to the fact that our mind is not conformed to the mind of God. Therefore, if we have a request to make, it might well be: "Let my mind, O Lord, be conformed to Thy mind, so that the two act as one".

April 11

Because our mind has to be changed, arguments with our soul may be helpful. For instance, we can point out, that because God is the good, then good only can come from him. Consequently, good only can come to us, no matter what the appearance of our present circumstance or experiences may be.

Because God, who is the good, is the only power and presence, evil cannot prevail. Good only can prevail, for good is the only power and presence.

April 12

Love keeps on being love – love to the uttermost. When we consider the matter, how great and wonderful is love! When we look back on our past life, we recognise with unspeakable gratitude that love has been with us all the way. Love has not failed us, although often we have failed love. In spite of all our unfaithfulness, love has always been faithful. No matter how far we have wandered, love still has loved us and been faithful, in spite of our unfaithfulness. It breaks our hearts when we remember how much we have failed, and yet how in spite of this, love has rescued us, forgiven us, restored us, and brought us to this present stage.

April 13

We can take each one about whom we are anxious and place them unreservedly in the love of God. No reservations – but just trust. If we make reservations or impose conditions, we restrict love; we hamper and limit God. What we have to do is simply to surrender ourselves, our will, our loved ones, our everything, to love. For when we surrender to love we surrender to God. And when we surrender to God, we surrender to infinite wisdom, for God is both love and wisdom. With love that is infinite, and wisdom that is infinite, how then can anything go wrong? How then can anything fail to be right?

April 14

Some people cannot think abstractly and cannot think of God as the one pervading spirit, but they can think of God, and love, personified in Jesus Christ. They can train themselves to think of Jesus being present with them. They can reserve a chair for him as the unseen guest. They can talk to him; tell him all their sorrows; share with him all their joys; confide in him all their hopes and aspirations. In course of time the presence of Jesus becomes such a reality that it is the most real part of their life.

April 15

There is a healing and restoring principle always functioning throughout the whole of nature. If we cut our finger, it begins to heal. All we have to do is draw the parts together and keep the cut clean. Nature does the rest ... but when we turn to the Lord in respect of really great troubles and upheavals, then higher laws are invoked and put in motion, which work to encompass our highest good.

These big experiences, these great and complicated problems, may take a long time to become adjusted. But if we turn constantly to the Lord, we put everything on the right basis, so that everything moves in a right direction. Each day brings us nearer to a state of adjustment, for the simple reason that we travel in the right direction through obeying divine law.

April 16

Because the matter is long drawn out, we may find our faith tested and tried. But this is only in order that we may learn to trust God in the dark as well as in the sunshine. A more severe test of our faith is when the experience begins to work out quite differently from what we may have hoped for and expected. But when this is so, we must not think that God is failing us. God may disappoint us over our small ideas of an adjustment, but, if he does so, it is only in order that a larger and better adjustment may be made possible.

April 17

We are so inclined to do too much ourselves. We want to do not only our own part, but also God's part. The very best work of healing is done by those who are able to stop the finite mind, so as to allow the mind of God to act without hindrance.

We are also far too anxious to see results. The essential thing is that we should turn to God, and continue to do so, for then we set in motion divine powers and potencies which possess the power to heal any situation and unravel the tangled skein of the most complicated circumstances.

April 18

If we have God's inward joy, then nothing else matters, and we possess that which is infinitely more valuable than all the riches contained in the whole world, and better far than any human harmony that we could imagine. A person might make their life the most harmonious and beautiful possible, so as to be the envy of all, yet if they did not know God's inward joy and peace, they would be a failure, and a mere beggar in the sight of heaven. They can know God's joy only to the extent that they know God. And when they know God, all things become possible, and they are on top of their life and on top of the world and all the experiences that life can bring.

April 19

If the disciples prayed that Jesus should be delivered from the chief priests, and allowed to go free, how disappointed they must have been when their Lord was crucified! Judging by appearances all was indeed lost. They had been taught by Jesus how to pray in such a way as to get results and even to move mountains by the exercise of faith, yet when a really great crisis had arisen these methods had failed signally. But had they failed signally? It is true that the crucifixion of Jesus had not been prevented, but in three days' time he rose from the dead.

So in like manner is it with our experiences. They may result in the burial of all our hopes, yet if we cling to truth and proclaim the goodness of life, we find that God has something better for us, and that all the time he has been working out for us all manner of good.

April 20

Gradually the light is coming to humankind; or rather, we are becoming increasingly aware of the light which has always been with us. We are becoming aware that we do not have to create perfection, for it is already with us, and that what has to be done is to remove the inhibitions, strain and distortion which cause an inversion. Owing to this inversion that which is inherently good becomes evil, just the opposite of what, inwardly, it really and truly is. In the future, true education will consist of methods which will be designed to remove these inhibitions and distortions, so that the divine perfection may appear.

April 21

The object of life is not to live a bovine kind of existence devoid of experience and adventure. The more the true aspirant advances, the more difficult become their problems and experiences. But if they will go forward, never looking back, they will become increasingly able to grapple with any situation. They learn by experience that though all things may seem to fail, yet God is always working out a perfect purpose.

April 22

Being born again means the incoming of the divine nature and the displacement of the old nature. Or, as some would prefer to say, it is the awakening in us of the divine nature which has been dormant hitherto. If we love the things of the Spirit and desire to follow a heavenly way of life, this proves that we have been born again from above, for the old human nature can never of itself experience any desire for God. If we possess any desire to know God, it is because the Spirit of God is already in us, and at work within us.

April 23

Reality, or heaven, is always present with us. It is round about us like an atmosphere. All the disorder around us is "heaven gone wrong", so to speak. Of course, heaven cannot go wrong, really, but we think unheavenly thoughts and feel unholy emotions, and these divorce us from the interior harmony and order. Heaven and its harmony are not changed. Our disharmony is due to the fact that we have stepped outside the divine order.

April 24

When once we have set out on the great adventure of treading the path of attainment, everything and every experience is divinely ordained to bring us nearer to the goal of divine union, which is a state of indescribable bliss. We find that God's hand is in everything, and that every experience is designed to bring us to our eternal joy. To realise this is a considerable step forward towards our goal; for the one who can see God everywhere and everything in God, and themself in God, and God in them, has already found God, although they have not yet found conscious unity with Him.

April 25

Each teacher is given a certain number of spiritual children for whom they are responsible, for whom they will have to give an account, and for whom they must be prepared to suffer. "To whom much is given, of them much shall be required." The one who scales a mountain does not expect the soft comforts of those who dwell in the valley. But then they could never tolerate the sheltered life of the valley. The call comes to dare all and to endure all, and they obey, for nothing less could ever satisfy their ardent soul.

April 26

"If God is omnipresent," it might be asked by some, "how is it He is nigh only to those who call upon Him?" The answer is that while it is true that God is present everywhere, as all-pervading Spirit, yet He does not become available to us until we turn to Him. We are surrounded by life-giving oxygen, yet until we breathe it into our lungs, it can do us no good. It is present with us, and we are immersed in it, yet for all the good we derive from it, it might just as well be absent.

April 27

It is much the same with us in a spiritual sense. We are surrounded by God, who is omnipresent Spirit, for "in Him we live and move, and have our being", yet, if we never pay Him any attention, if we ignore Him, and treat Him as though there were no God, then we cut ourselves off from His love and care.

How different it is when we turn to the Lord and call upon Him! In so doing we recognise and acknowledge God, and also put ourselves in the right position for the power, wisdom and love of God to operate in our life.

April 28

The great and wise Emerson said: "Place yourself in the middle of the stream of power and wisdom which flows into you as life; place yourself in the full centre of the flood; then you are without effort impelled to truth, to right, and a perfect contentment."

By constant prayer, through continually looking to our divine centre, we are kept in the middle of the stream of life, and in course of time we realise that really and truly, deep down in our inmost being and essence, we truly are that life.

And so, we come to know the glorious truth which can never be described or defined, and which can only be experienced. Then the truth makes us free, even as Jesus promised that it should do so.

April 29

If we would get beyond the human intellect to that which is beyond all form and idea, we have to reach out to the formless. By turning to that which is beyond all human understanding, an inward awareness grows up within us which is quite apart from intellectual understanding. There is a perfection which is beyond perfection, a wholeness which is beyond wholeness, and order which is beyond order. All that we can see or know is but an imperfect reflection, or appearance, of the hidden perfection which is invisible.

April 30

In order to help another, it is necessary to retire into the secret place, making contact with our divine source, and then see with the eye of faith the whole matter as it is in God. We see, without strain or effort, the perfect healing or divine adjustment as already accomplished in the love and mercy of God. We reject all negative appearance as being not true of the true person or child of God, and concentrate, calmly and without strain, upon the divine wholeness and perfection which are the truth.

CHAPTER FIVE

May

May 1

Certain seers and others who claim to possess a knowledge of the spiritual world tell us that if a denizen wants to converse with another denizen, they do not have to travel through space, but the one they desire to speak to immediately appears. It is said that the modern craze for speed on this earth plane is a counterfeit of the true, effortless, instantaneous movement of heaven.

If we think lofty thoughts, use heavenly words (love, joy, peace, harmony, order, perfection, etc.) then we become surrounded by a heavenly host who stand back of such words.

May 2

We possess a deeper life, or a deeper life possesses us, which connects us with the Infinite and gives us entrance to the eternal. As we breathe the cosmic breath, or when it breathes through us, our life expands until it embraces the whole creation and that which is beyond. It is when our breathing becomes attuned to the breathing of the divine Spirit that we "know" that which is beyond knowing. In this cosmic awareness, the soul realises itself and enters into "the glorious liberty of the children of God".

May 3

Sometimes it seems that we are being led by a very strange path, and it may seem all wrong to us, but this is because we see only the outside of things. The eye of omniscience, however, sees everything, and omniscient Mind knows everything; consequently, we are guided by a way which, although unknown to us, is known always to the mind of God.

> I will bring the blind by a way they know not; I will lead them in paths that they have not known; I will make darkness light before them, and crooked places straight.
>
> Isaiah 42:16

May 4

At the present time, when we are all faced with we know not what, when established institutions are crumbling and life on this planet entirely changed, we need to be established in that which is unchanging and immutable. The old hymn-writer struck a pessimistic note in the words: "Change and decay in all around I see."

We, in a later and far more important and critical age, look around us and see change, and more rapid and far-reaching changes than the world has ever seen before, but we do not see decay. Far from it. What we see are the cracks in the old order which is giving place to the new. What we are experiencing is the influx of new life which is splitting up the old, even as new wine would split old wine skins.

May 5

So long as those in authority deal with present trouble in the way of the lower person, just so long will trouble, disorder and unrest continue to appear. Let us pray, therefore, for those who govern the nations of the world, that they may be given spiritual insight and spiritual understanding, so that they may do those things which are according to divine law.

May 6

We are all members one of another, so that by our identification with the real spiritual self we can help to raise others also. We cannot live to ourselves alone. Everything that we do has its effect upon other people, and the world as a whole. By realising our true state of oneness with the Eternal we help to raise others to the same level. This demands of us persistence and perseverance. It is not for ourselves alone that we work, nor for our nation alone, but for the benefit of all life.

May 7

What we desire for ourselves, if we were to secure it, might prove to be very different from what we fondly imagined it would be, and there might be many undesirable drawbacks which we had never imagined would be possible. These, of course, would destroy our happiness and peace.

But when infinite wisdom conceives a thing, it contains none of these drawbacks. "The blessing of the Lord, it makes rich, and He adds no sorrow with it." If we pray for a divine adjustment according to infinite wisdom and love, then the adjustment, when it comes, is so perfect that we find no sorrow added, and no disadvantages to mar our joy.

May 8

The Kingdom of God is that state of consciousness in which we realise that a divine adjustment exists everywhere. The divine will and the divine order are everywhere present. What has been accomplished has been that we have been brought back to union with the divine order. The only change has been in us, not in God, nor in God's will or mind. God is always the same. He is the joy that is beyond joy, the peace beyond all peace, the satisfaction beyond all satisfaction.

May 9

Everything that we can ever need is already ours in the mind of God. The pattern or archetype is there, and we can reproduce it in the world which we know and normally function in — according to our faith. If we exercise a little faith, it is as though we take a teacup to the ocean of blessedness. But if we exercise a larger faith, it is as though we took a bucket to be filled. If we exercise a still greater faith, it is as though we took a travelling tank. God's supply is infinite and inexhaustible.

May 10

In the same way that God's infinite life is inexhaustible, knowing no weariness nor decay, being self-renewing from within itself, and always in a state of perfect prime, so also is the bounty or substance of God — it can never become impoverished or lessened in the slightest degree. Its riches can never fade away.

It is to this God to whom we have access.

May 11

It is when we cease to be self-centred that we are set free. Praying always for our own healing prevents the blessing from coming to us. "It is more blessed to give than to receive," said Jesus. It is more blessed to pray for the healing of others than it is to pray for our own healing. By giving we become liberated; by praying for others, we become blessed, even as we would that they should be blessed.

This is the law of life which Jesus taught.

May 12

As the atom is a replica in miniature of the solar universe, so also is each person a replica in miniature of God. God is the macrocosm, while the human being is the microcosm. A dewdrop reflects the full-orbed glory of the sun. In the same way we can reflect God by being attuned to Him.

When we come into tune with the Eternal, the peace of God flows through us. All that we do, really, is to find God's inward peace, for when we experience His peace, it is because we have found God.

May 13

What people are really afraid of is the unknown. They can face any trouble on land or sea and meet with equanimity "the slings and arrows of outrageous fortune," but they fear to step out into the unknown. We can call the bluff of this fear, by actually doing the thing of which we are afraid. But we cannot do this alone. We can only do it as we go forward, taking hold of God's hand, so to speak, stepping out into the void, with nothing under our feet. If we do this, then we find that under our feet is the rock which can never fail, and that we are brought through the darkness into God's marvellous light. We also experience such a revelation of God as

Love, and such a sense of union with Him, that we can never fear the unknown again.

May 14

Some people are very afraid of becoming merged into the One. They want to remain acorns always. Yet the acorn when it becomes a tree, if it could think, would find itself an expression of the one life which brings forth all trees. Those who are afraid of becoming merged into the One Life, God, are already so merged, only they are not aware of it.

May 15

Really and truly, we are one with the Eternal. Our soul is omnipresent and can visit all places, and in a moment of time. Just as wireless waves come through walls and through our body, so does the Eternal Spirit sweep through us. There is no line of separation or demarcation: we are one.

We live in two worlds at one and the same time. Outwardly we live the narrow, confined, time-space, three-dimensional life of the senses. Inwardly our soul occupies or pervades the timeless, spaceless, unlimited Eternal.

May 16

It sometimes happens that when I look up in the sky, I can see a background of high cloud so distant as to appear stationary, while before it pass rapidly low clouds which hide the distant sky from view while they pass between me and it. The distant, motionless sky gives me a thrill as I gaze at it, for it symbolises the unchanging reality. The low clouds which obscure but for a moment represent the changing scenes, difficulties and temporary experiences of life. As I keep my sight fixed upon the motionless high sky, the quickly passing low clouds become a mere transient trifle. I experience a feeling of oneness with reality, of being at the centre of all things, and one with it.

May 17

Much harm can be done by self-condemnation. We can hold ourselves under a sort of curse through persisting in this practice. Whenever we think of a wrong we have done in the past which makes us feel as though we can never forgive ourselves for it, we should confess it to God and leave the matter in His hands for Him to overrule it for good and bring about a divine adjustment. Or we can declare that we have already confessed our wrongdoing, and that God has forgiven us. Of course, we should make restitution where we can, but if this is not possible, we can give our best to others in general, so as to repay our debt to life so far as it is possible for us to do so.

May 18

If our life was going to be taken from us and someone intervened and saved us, or if we were going to be sold up and evicted, and someone came along and paid the rent for us, how grateful we should be! How earnest and fervent would be our thanks to our benefactor. Our words of gratitude would be filled with the power of our very heart and soul.

In the same way, as we praise, bless and thank the Lord, we must put all the intensity of which we are capable into our words, so that they become filled with power.

I believe it is possible to praise ourselves out of almost any dilemma. Praising God does not alter His mind, will or attitude towards us, but it alters us, so that we become a positive magnet of attraction, towards which all manner of divine good tends to gravitate.

May 19

A destructive habit to which most of us, alas, are only too prone is that of fearing the future. The human mind races on ahead in its fear of something which seems to be threatening us, and then if that happens, we imagine further disasters involving us or our loved ones. So, the mind deals in a panicky way with things which will never happen.

This may be checked by using the statement: "God is in the midst of this experience." Some may say they cannot do this because they have no such understanding, and such a statement conveys nothing to them. In spite of that they still might use it, for if they make use of words of truth, they will be helped by them, because such words have power, whether they are understood or not. Indeed, it is through the use of such statements of truth that many people enter into an understanding or realisation of the words they utter.

May 20

Now, at this present moment, it is possible for us to wing our way to the stars: to experience that state of bliss described in the book of Job: "When the morning stars sang together, and all the sons of God shouted for joy." The world of reality is perfect and lovely beyond compare. To this real world of fadeless beauty, we belong. It is our privilege as children to mount up with wings as eagles and to know the reality which is everlasting rightness and joy unspeakable.

May 21

The divine principle is not recognised by the world, hence the disorder of the world. We can help by recognising and acknowledging the divine principle of order, wholeness and perfection continually. It has been said that the safety of a nation depends on the number of its contemplatives. By contemplatives is meant those people who have found God and can stand in the divine light, radiance and glory. Given a sufficient number of these, a nation would become immune from all attacks upon its integrity, both from without and from within.

May 22

If we make friends with life and enter into fellowship with the interior order which holds the whole universe together in harmony and oneness, then when "the evil time" comes, we are maintained in a wonderful manner. We must not claim, however, that this is due to any merit on our part, or to any particular system or technique, or to our faithfulness in prayer, or to our perseverance in meditation, or indeed to anything that we do ourselves, but we must acknowledge that all the wonderful support and blessing in difficult times which comes to us are from God alone.

May 23

The prayer life is a progressive unfoldment of understanding of God and leads us to that state spoken of by John: "And this is life eternal, that they might know Thee, the only true God." It begins with seeking: it ends in knowing. In order to know God, we have to become one with Him – in a state of unison or union. When we reach this point we enter into God's inward peace, and it is not possible to experience this until we become at-oned with Him…

If we want to experience God in the external life, we must find Him in the interior life. First within, then without. Although God is everywhere, yet it is only in the deepest recesses of our soul that we can really find Him.

May 24

When a door begins to close, unless we know better, we naturally try, by every means in our power, to prevent it from closing. We may try everything in a practical way, such as writing letters, interviewing people of influence, and so on.

Also, we pray most vehemently that the door should not close. The result of all this being that we may become ill, beside making ourselves unhappy and worried. Yet in spite of all our efforts the door closes.

But, while this is taking place, another door is opening for us, but we may not be aware of it, simply because we are so busily engaged in struggling against the closing of the other door. Fighting against life's experiences is not only a waste of energy, it also distracts our attention, so that we fail to see the new door of opportunity as it opens before us.

May 25

If we retire from the world of cares and worries in order to live a life of calm contemplation, we may be disappointed. I know that some of the greatest saints lived in this way, and I love them, pray for them, and salute them. But the vast majority of people will, I feel sure, make better progress by living a life of love and service in this workaday world. Every trial, every experience, brings us nearer to the heart of God, while every obstacle is turned into a stepping stone to higher and better things. At the end of a difficult experience, we always find ourselves advanced yet another step in our journey back to God. The greater and more challenging the experience, the bigger the step forward. When we look back, we acknowledge that the way has been rough, but we declare that it has been worthwhile, and we would not have had it otherwise.

May 26

Of course, we can run into quite a lot of trouble through neglect of our private devotions and spiritual exercises. It is so much easier to read a religious book or newspaper, or go to a religious meeting, than to engage in private prayers or devotions. But these can never take the place of retiring to the secret place and communing with the unseen.

If we practise this, then in addition, during the day, we can make contact with our divine source, while still engaged in dealing with the practical affairs of life. Everything we do can be made a subject of prayer. We can pray to God before commencing every duty, before keeping an appointment, or while we are waiting for an interview, or before writing a sentence.

May 27

No one can become a saint all at once. It is a process of growth, and it takes time. The pilgrim should not be too discouraged when the old nature comes to the top, and they find themselves just where they started. As a matter of fact, they appear to be back at the old spot from which they started the journey, yet actually they are a turn of the spiral higher than before.

May 28

One of the greatest discoveries that we make in the course of our journey through time and space, is that God is at work in our life, and that He is dealing with us in a personal and intimate way, just as though we were the only being in the universe. And what is true of us must be true of all our fellows, for God is no respecter or discriminator of persons – He loves us all equally and without limit.

For many years we may think we are friendless and alone, and that "it all depends on us." For many years we may think we are turning the world round, and that we have to bear the burdens of the world. Then, after many experiences, we may suddenly realise that God is at work in the world, and in our life and affairs, and in the lives and affairs of all people.

May 29

When we were young, we may have been taught that God is a hard taskmaster and someone to be feared. But I have found through experience that God is quite different. I have found Him to be Love without any reservation or limit. I was taught that God always had His eye on me, so that if I did anything wrong, He would punish me. But my experience of God is that He is absolute Love, and that He pursues us down the years, not to punish us but in order to love and bless us.

May 30

When we know the truth about God – that He is infinite Love and Wisdom, always seeking to make us happy and to bless us in every possible way – our thinking about God becomes right thinking, whereas formerly it was wrong thinking. When we think of God as Love, we think rightly of Him because that is the truth about His nature. Therefore, because we think according to truth, our thinking is right thinking. If, however, we think of God as one to be feared, we think according to error; thus, our thinking is wrong thinking and based on a lie.

May 31

Over the Delphic temple were the words: "Man, know thyself." Knowing ourselves means discovering our true nature – outwardly, our natural body; inwardly, our soul which gives life to the body, and which can breathe and eat and drink apart from the body, as well as think, see and hear; and, most interior of all, spirit which is part of the one universal Spirit, which knows no beginning or ending, never has been sick, and which never has sinned. Thus, interiorly, we are one with the Eternal.

CHAPTER SIX

June

June 1

Security cannot be found by seeking for it, or by playing for safety. Life calls for bold and constructive action. If we hold in our mind a concept of something finer and better than our present stage of attainment, then we will always move forward and upward. Circumstances may change and material things pass away, but the creative idea in our mind will remain. This creative idea will always bring forth fruit in our life after its kind.

If, therefore, our mind is stayed upon God, who is infinite substance and creativeness, the one source of all visible (and also invisible) manifestation, then our life becomes stable and secure. That is the only security.

June 2

God's peace and the bliss of union did not come to me as a result of practising any particular form of prayer or technique. It is true

I may have drunk at what I thought were "many fountains", but only in order that I might discover through experience that instead of being fountains, they were only broken cisterns. Then, when I least expected it, the heavenly gift came. So, then I knew that what used to be termed the gift of the Holy Ghost, comes not as a reward of much strenuous effort, but that it glides into our soul, imperceptibly, like the rising of the sun on a spring morning.

June 3

True healing comes like the rising of the sun on a spring morning also, in a perfectly harmonious fashion. There is no strain or resistance. The disease fades away in the same way that darkness disappears at the approach of dawn. We cannot explain it; all that we know is that it has come to us and set us free.

Healing, like most things, is better if we allow it to come to us in a divinely natural way, at the proper time. True healing is subtle and cannot be described or understood. We may desire it for years, and try all manner of prayer, without achieving any good result. Then, when we're off our guard, and thinking about, and attending to, something else, healing comes quietly and unannounced.

June 4

Those who follow this teaching, which is a return to the teachings of Jesus, may meet with opposition from those who are still in a straitjacket of conformity, and who very much resent any ideas which are new to them. The rule is never to argue, and always to let them have their own way. We should never argue. We should retire into strength and pray that those who criticise and misrepresent us should be divinely blessed in every possible way and prospered according to heavenly standards. We should also pray that whatever may be amiss in ourselves may be corrected.

June 5

As many of us are aware, people are a microcosm of the macrocosm: each one is a replica of the universe. In them are what correspond to the sun, moon, stars and planets. If we follow Jesus, the spirit of Jesus will rule our planets and suns and all our being.

In other words, we become integrated. That is, we conform to the divine pattern of our life. Psychologists term it reorganising the personality. Evangelicals call it becoming sanctified. We would prefer to call it a divine adjustment through surrender. As soon as we cease distorting our life and personality by working against the divine pattern, everything springs back into its proper place, so to speak. As I have often said: if we squeeze a tennis ball, it becomes distorted and is no longer round. Directly we cease to squeeze it, it springs back to its proper shape and becomes a true sphere again. We do not have to make it so; it becomes so of itself, because it has been designed and made in a truly spherical form.

June 6

We give up the self-righteous idea that we are right and our enemy wrong, that we are good, and they are wicked. Consequently, we no longer want them altered, because we realise that we may be the ones who need altering, and so we simply pray that they may be blessed in every possible way. In other words, when we love our enemy enough, then we do not want them altered, but rather do we pray that we may be altered, so that we can no longer see their wrong points, but only their many good qualities. Love is the key to every situation in life.

June 7

If our loved ones are not manifesting the harmony that we should like to see, we should not be too perturbed about it. God's pattern is there, but they have not yet learned to follow it. Let us take comfort from the fact that God is at work in their lives just as He is and has been in ours. He is just as interested in their lives as He is in ours, and Love is waiting on them just as Love has waited on us, all our life's journey.

In spite of this knowledge, we must not cease to pray. Also, we must not give up praying because we see no result of our prayers.

June 8

When we pray, however, we should not be coercive. We should neither attempt to coerce God by our importunities, nor dominate those for whom we pray by our self-will. We should pray not that they act according to the way we think they ought to act. We should give them complete liberty. Also, we must give God perfect liberty, so that we do not limit His working in their lives, even as He has worked in ours.

June 9

Looking back, in an understanding way, explains many of our so-called failures. In my own case, I can see many failures that were necessary. If I had been successful at the time, it would have been a hindrance instead of a gain. If I had been able to make a material success of every one of my early efforts, I should have remained in the rut of circumstances all my life.

Instead of being allowed to go our own way, which would have led to real failure and frustration, we were happily restrained, after which a much better way was opened before us, which led to joy and full self-expression.

June 10

In order to be led by the Spirit we have to be surrendered to the will of the Spirit. This we should have no hesitation in doing, for the Spirit knows all things. It knows now, at this moment, what is happening everywhere, and also what will be happening in, say, half an hour's time, when we are in the midst of dense traffic, or maybe taking off at an aerodrome, or descending in a pit shaft in a cage, or cutting a piece of bread in the home. If we are led and guided by the Spirit, we do everything at the right moment, so that we and everything else are in the right place, in a state of order and harmony.

June 11

One who surrenders to the Spirit, giving up their "self" in order that the Spirit may use them, may have, and most probably will have, other opportunities of being filled with the Spirit—until they become a Spirit-filled person.

Such men and women bring the presence of God with them wherever they go. The light of Heaven shines from their faces, and everyone who is attuned is conscious of it. When they speak of the love of God, and His dealings with them, their faces light up, as though with a hidden flame. And those who come in contact with them are encouraged and blessed and filled with a great peace.

June 12

In our usual state of ordinary human consciousness, we are, as it were, fixed in a shell of illusion, much in the same way that a chick is imprisoned within the shell of the egg in which it has gradually grown up. And, just as the chick by constant pecking finally cracks the shell open and steps out of darkness and imprisonment into a light and radiant world of movement and freedom, so also do we, when our consciousness, through prayer and meditation, expands beyond its present limitation, step out into a new and infinite world.

June 13

Most of us are debtors and not creditors of life. We owe life such a lot. We are indebted for so many blessings, and yet we do nothing in return, and perhaps do not give even one word of gratitude, praise, or thanks to God for all His mercies. We receive, but we do not give. Consequently, our account is overdrawn. We have drawn out too much and have paid too little in. Consequently, our life is empty and unblessed.

June 14

We should become creditors of life, instead of debtors. I do not think we shall succeed, but we can all try to give more to life than we take out. It has been said we only get out of life what we put in. How much better it would be if we could put more into life than we take out! Personally, I have never been able to do this, for the more I give—and it has been little enough—the more I receive. "Give, and it shall be given you; good measure, pressed down, and shaken together, and running over, shall people give into your bosom."

June 15

Serving others does not mean that we are to become interfering busybodies, trying to convert people to our way of thinking and living. What is required of us is to remove the beam from our own eye, instead of trying to remove the splinter from our brother's eye. We have to put ourselves right with life and restore the balance, before we are capable of instructing others as to what they should do, or what they should not do. Let them be guided by our example, rather than by what we say.

June 16

We must not think that we have to create a state of blessedness by our own efforts, for it already exists; in fact, it is a reality. All states of unblessedness are a departure from the real and permanent state of blessedness. This is a state of balance, and it is waiting to be restored in our life as soon as ever the conditions are fulfilled. We do not have to create good, which is a state of balance, for good already *is*. What we term evil is really a departure from the good, a state of unbalance.

Yet we have to make a channel for it, so that it can manifest. This is accomplished through prayer, and by prayer I mean waiting upon God and becoming attuned to the divine note. If we stay our mind upon God, then gradually our discordant note gives place to the divine note—the grand *Amen*, forever sounding throughout eternity.

June 17

Those who are possessed by a great desire to serve and want to accomplish as much as possible are apt to fall into the temptation to be all Martha and no Mary. They are tempted to work instead of pray, at the expense of the prayer life. For the sake of the work, they must insist upon being Mary, for a time, each day. Those who neglect prayer in order to do more work find themselves enmeshed in an increasing multitude of feverish activities which take an increasing toll of their strength. But one who makes a point of waiting upon God is able to do much more work than the "busy" one who is too hard-worked to pray, while the work that they do is of a different quality; it is effective and its results are enduring.

June 18

No one can explain what God's peace is. It transcends all words, but it fills us with bliss and joy.

If we possess the peace of God, we possess everything. If we have not the peace of God, we possess nothing. So long as we possess the peace of God, we are happy and filled with the joys of Heaven. If we lose God's peace, we are miserable.

Although we cannot define God's inward peace, yet we can carry it with us, so that other people, who are ready for it, can become conscious of it. Just as some people carry trouble wherever they go, they who are filled with God's peace bring a sense of calm.

June 19

Why should those who give up their all, in order to put the quest before everything else, have to pass through tormenting experiences, through times of anguish, while those who only make use of God's powers for their own self-interest have a comparatively good time?

In our eagerness we press on so fast that we enter a realm for which we are not yet quite prepared. Swedenborg speaks of spirits belonging to a lower plane wanting to go to a heavenly one, and that when their wish was granted, they were so tormented by the love, joy, peace and loveliness of Heaven that they begged to be taken back to an environment more suited to their inward state. It was the visitors' lack of correspondence with the heavenly vibrations which caused their suffering.

It is the same with us. These painful experiences are due entirely to the vibrations of divine love being too high and powerful for us, but the very experiences themselves change us, so that we become adapted to the new conditions. As soon as this is achieved, we enter into a measure of God's peace.

June 20

We can attain only if we are prepared to go all the way with Jesus, instead of only part of the way. There are many who are willing to go with Him as far as Gethsemane, but there, like the disciples, they fall asleep, and that is as far as they get.

Their religion is really an attempt to avoid what I have termed redemptive tribulation. They are willing to go with Him, so long as He provides the loaves and fishes, and heals their sicknesses. But when they discover that His kingdom is a spiritual one, and not material, they walk no more with Him. Or should they find themselves at Gethsemane, they forsake Him and flee from Him.

June 21

The reward, over the years, of tests and trials is that we reach that state when God's peace is always with us. If a disturbing experience should rob us of our peace, it is quickly restored. This is because to be in God's peace has become the normal condition for us; consequently, it is natural for peace to be restored. If we throw a stone into a pond, the surface is rippled, but soon it becomes smooth again, because it is normal to be smooth.

June 22

We should not grieve too much when our loved ones pass on. Neither should we be anxious about them if they did not accept the doctrine which certain people tell us is necessary. They will find themselves in just that environment which suits perfectly their present stage of unfoldment, and which will enable them to make progress towards higher and better things.

God is Infinite Love and Infinite Wisdom; consequently, everything has been arranged exactly right for each one of us, no matter at what stage we may be. God has a place for each one of us, and that place is perfect.

June 23

As we sit or lie in the great stillness, we realise that God, the One Universal Spirit, is all around us, and that the beams of the one life are flowing through us. And this, in turn, makes the body less material.

In the ordinary way, in the rush and activity, always striving to do more work and yet more work, we seem to have no time for waiting on the Lord; consequently, the true pattern of our life cannot appear, nor of our body.

Therefore, let us draw apart from the stress and strain of life, and rest a while. Let us realise that the rays and beams of the One Universal, Everlasting Life are penetrating and flowing through us, changing our material body into the likeness and substance of Itself—Spirit.

June 24

It is all the work of the Spirit, who brings us just what we need, when we are ready for it. It is the Spirit who guides us as we write, and it is the same Spirit who thrills the reader when they read what has been written...

Sometimes the recipient of a letter has testified to receiving, as it were, a baptism of God's peace, lasting for several days. They have been inclined to attribute it to something I have done… but it is a sort of replica of the peace which was in my heart at the time of writing. If I had not experienced God's peace when writing, then the recipient would have had no realisation of God's peace when reading. It was due to the One Spirit being in both of us, which made the realisation of God's peace possible.

June 25

God is calling each one of us, and within each one of us is something which responds. This "something" within us is not, however, always ready to respond. We have to pass through what is termed the awakening stage. We have to be quickened. The dead have to be raised. All the experiences of life, especially its frustrations, wear away the wrapping which covers up the Divine Light within us, until at last, generally after many tribulations, we become aware of our true identity.

June 26

Nowadays, my delight is to speak of the joys of the Spirit. The highest earthly joys and bliss are but a counterfeit of the real joys and bliss which become ours when, having become quickened by the Spirit, we enter into a state of Divine Union.

Heaven is generally spoken of as a place of exterior beauty and harmony. But actually, it is an interior state. Heaven consists of those who love the things of the Spirit... it is an outward expression of the love, joy, peace, harmony and bliss which are within our own soul.

June 27

The Divine pattern of our life is that we should manifest "perfect everything". We possess the power within us to manifest according to the Divine pattern. It is not the feeble power of the finite personality; it is the power of the Infinite, which will work through us if we recognise and believe in it.

It does not matter how great our difficulties may be, nor how complicated our circumstances, the power within is capable of overcoming the greatest of difficulties and unravelling the tangled skein of our life. For the inward power is also Infinite Wisdom and Intelligence.

June 28

It is a well-known truth that only like can see like, and that only God can see God. We, ourselves, cannot see God at all. In fact, we have no desire whatever either to know God, or to see God. We are quite incapable of having the slightest interest in God.

But there is something in us which can respond to God and vibrate in correspondence with the Divine. Just at the right time this becomes awakened and quickened in us. This something which is born or awakened in us is the son of God. And it is this God in us which is capable of knowing God. We, of ourselves, cannot know God, but the son of God within us is capable of doing so.

June 29

There are times when we are given cosmic insight. Our consciousness expands until it seems to embrace the whole universe. It seems as though we are at the top of a mountain, while before us lies stretched out the heaving mass of humanity, and we are filled with a great pity and compassion. We can understand the words of Jesus: "Come unto me, all ye that are weary... and I will give you rest." And also, the words of John: "Love not the world, neither the things that are in the world... the world passeth away, and the lust thereof; but they that doeth the will of God abideth forever."

June 30

Nowadays, thanks be, my life and my surroundings are normally filled with light; and often I find the common everyday things around me looking strangely beautiful. Not only flowers, which seem able to transport me into another world, but also common articles take upon themselves a beauty and a glory not their own. From this it would appear that, to a certain extent, metaphysicians are right when they declare that beauty is more in our own soul than in the objects around us.

Chapter Seven

July

July 1

A caterpillar is very different from a butterfly, but it is the same creature. If we were to call a certain caterpillar by the name of Samuel, then when he became a chrysalis, he would still be Samuel, and also when he emerged from the chrysalis as a butterfly, he would still be Samuel. When we find God and enter into union, we do not become dissolved... but instead, our consciousness expands until it embraces the whole and, so it seems, is the whole. This, however, is a great mystery, and it cannot be encompassed by the reasoning mind.

July 2

If a person of prayer is in great trouble, they do not talk about it or worry over it, but they set themselves to earnest, fervent prayer. They keep on praying believingly until all at once they know that what they are praying for is an accomplished fact. They not only believe that they have, but they know that they have. After that, their prayer takes the form of thanksgiving.

July 3

Of course, we must pray within the will of God. If, when we pray, we begin to feel that it is not the best thing we are praying for, then we should refrain from forcing matters, praying instead for guidance and for God to deal with the matter in His own way and at His own time.

We should not try to force our mind patterns onto God, but should pray that His perfect mind patterns be revealed in us.

July 4

With regard to the problem of evil. As our readers have been taught, Reality is a state of wholeness and completeness, in which everything is in its right place at the right time. And everything remains right so long as every part is in its right place. But, owing to our departure from the original unity and order, what is termed evil appears. For what was good when in its right place and performing its right uses becomes destructive and disorderly when it leaves its right place and ceases its right uses. The work of God (Holy Spirit, Christ, or Lord) in our heart is to bring us back to the original order and state of unity and completeness.

July 5

The best work is done without strain, and with great ease, freedom and enjoyment. The reason is, of course, that inspiration comes from the real and true world, which is the perfect expression of the Divine Idea.

In the real world everything is done without effort or strain. Our efforts in this material world are but a counterfeit of the real effortless accomplishment of the real and perfect. The present-day craze for speed, for instance, which not only enslaves us but threatens to destroy us all—this also is but a counterfeit of what takes place in the real world, where everything happens with the speed of thought.

July 6

It seems rather late in the day, seeing that humankind has almost ruined this fair earth, but if people were to turn to God, I am sure that a wonderful and quick recovery would take place. And by this I do not mean that we should follow messages from the "other side", as it is called. What I mean is that we should seek true inspiration, not from any plane, but direct from the mind of God.

July 7

Prayer ushers us into a new world which awaits our exploration. Humankind has explored outwardly and has brought the world to the brink of disaster. Now, if we explore inwardly, we will find harmony, order, and perfect everything.

People have sought in every place but the right one, and the more they have sought, the farther away from happiness they have wandered. Now, if they will look within and turn to their Divine Source, they will find joy and peace.

July 8

At the right moment the call comes for us to come up higher. "When that which is perfect is come, then that which is in part shall be done away." All that we have achieved, though good up to a point and perfect as far as it goes, is found to be "only in part". But when "that which is perfect is come", then what we have achieved is seen to be only a beginning, a stepping stone, a preparation for higher things.

July 9

It makes a great difference if we realise we are not alone, and that God is sharing life's difficult experiences with us. You can say to yourself: "Because God is with me, I cannot be afraid." Also, you can declare: "God is with me in this experience, and He is Love. God is also behind this experience; therefore, in spite of appearances, it can only be Love."

July 10

My experience has been that we enter into God's peace, and it enters into us, after we have passed through great trial and torment of soul... when we reach this stage, we realise that our true life is rooted in God, and that it has infinite extensions beyond time and space. Realising this ushers us into a new world—a world of infinite extensions. Time and space are transcended, and we find ourselves at the Centre, while nations, so it seems, rise and fall, and universes come into being and then pass away. Our breathing becomes deep and rhythmic, in tune with the hidden life. Our soul breathes the finer ethers of the Life of God.

July 11

So many of us do not yet realise that the cause of most of the disharmony in our life is due to our own sourness, or what is sometimes described as "prickliness". The trouble is within ourselves and we see it reflected in others. The reason we criticise others is that we see reflected in them our own faults and unpleasant qualities. It is only Divine love flowing through us that can put us right. It is the only cure, so I have found, for what is termed a difficult temperament.

July 12

I have heard of well-meaning people who have worn themselves out and had breakdowns through trying to heal others. This was because they tried to do it themselves, instead of relying on the powers of the Name. They identified themselves with the sufferer instead of invoking the all-powerful Name.

Therefore, those who attempt to do healing should do so in the name of Jesus, at the same time disassociating themselves and their own efforts from the act of healing, leaving it entirely to the power of the Name. Then they will suffer from no depletion.

July 13

When we pray, we should not try to compel anything to happen, either good or bad, but only to find God, who transcends what we know as good or bad. Prayer raises us up above the pairs of opposites to the midpoint where all conflicting forces are reconciled and only a state of wholeness or oneness obtains.

Prayer, so far from being a strain, should be relaxation. It is our strained, anxious state of mind which separates us from God. When we relax, we resume that state spoken of in Genesis as the image and likeness of God.

July 14

Perfection already is, and always has been. This is why Jesus taught us to pray: "Thy Kingdom come, Thy will be done on earth as it is in Heaven." God's will is perfect everything, so that all we need is that God's will should be done.

Of course, we still have to live in the pairs of opposites, but all disharmonies can be dispersed by rising above them to the midpoint where we find God's inward peace.

July 15

There are times in the lives of all of us when the rhythm of life is broken by loss or bereavement, or when for some other reason we may be reduced to a state of extremity. When all may seem lost and our position desperate, then it is we are raised up by a Power greater than our own, and set at liberty, with all our wants supplied.
When deliverance comes, that is, a deliverance which is spiritual emancipation, it is wonderful how quickly our circumstances become changed. The whole picture of our life becomes transformed like a dissolving view change of picture in the old-fashioned magic lantern. In those days we children would see a picture on the screen. Then it would become blurred and still more blurred, until much to our surprise a new picture would arise out of the indistinct mixture. In the same way our own circumstances can change just as completely.

July 16

It is important that we should apply what we read to our own soul and our own experience. As soon as we find ourselves thinking — that is just what so-and-so needs, or that would make the subject of a good sermon — we should apply it to ourselves instead. It is we who need the instruction; it is we who need to put it into practice.

July 17

She said: "The great thing is to realise and experience the presence of God and after that nothing else matters." When she uttered those simple words, it was as though an electric shock passed through me. In that moment I stepped out into Eternity. It was like stepping out of a frame or doorway into limitless being. All limitations fell away, and at once I was perfectly at home in God. Infinite power surged through me and seemed to fill the place, which also seemed filled with glory.

These things come to us when we least expect them. A few simple words, and lo, in the twinkling of an eye, we are changed. When we try for them, they elude us. It is when we are not trying and when we are off our guard — it is then that we find our true place in God. It is then that the Invasion of the Eternal takes place.

July 18

It seems that, as a result of meditation, a higher or spiritual mind opens and begins to function — a mind which grasps deep spiritual truths without having to reason. It has direct knowledge. Being a spiritual mind, it knows spiritual truths intuitively. It recognises them as those things which have always been known and said. This explains what St Paul meant when he said that spiritual things must be spiritually discerned, because the carnal mind cannot understand or know the deep things of God.

July 19

If we pray in a possessive way, we only make life more difficult for the one for whom we pray. In prayer we make use of the most powerful of all the imponderable forces. By possessive or directive prayer we try to put our loved one into a straitjacket of our own devising. Each one must be allowed to live their life in their own way. God is at work in the life of each one of us; therefore, we must not only allow freedom and liberty to the one for whom we pray, but also we must allow freedom and liberty to God, so that He can deal with them in His own way.

July 20

There is another reason why we should not pray for others to be changed. The cause of all the trouble may be in ourselves. We must be willing to admit this, but that is the last thing some of us are willing to do... We may be seeing our own inward maladjustments reflected in the lives of others.
If we feel we must pray for something, let us pray for a divine adjustment. That allows God to adjust us, as well as other people.

July 21

The very fact that you have a desire to help others shows that the Divine Spirit is at work in you. When you become quickened yourself, others may be quickened when you pray for them...
Ask in the name of Jesus. Our church prayers are asked for the

sake of, and not in. But Jesus said that if we asked in His name our prayers would be answered: "Whatsoever you shall ask in my name, that will I do."

When we pray in the name which is above every name, we should remember that we, of ourselves, can do nothing, but that the power which heals and restores is in the Name.

July 22

The life of the Spirit is one of progress. We must not stand still. We must not remain in petrified and crystallised ideas that belong to a dead past. We must break new ground: we must open our minds to new ideas, or what to us may seem new ideas, but which are neither new nor old. They are facets of eternal truth which always has been and which always will be. Absolute truth cannot change, for it is the same yesterday, today and forever. It is we who change: it is we who must change. We cannot stand still: we must unfold like a flower. But we cannot do this if we do not accept what appears to us to be new ideas.

July 23

We have only to keep going in order to become victorious in life's journey. Things are so arranged that we can always win through, and indeed cannot fail to do so, if we go forward in faith. The only one who can defeat us is ourselves… No person and no circumstance can compel us to be beaten. If we put our trust in God's promises, believing them to be true, then our courage is maintained, and we become filled with renewed strength and power. The statement is forever true: "Great your strength, if great your need."

July 24

People sometimes write to me asking why I do not teach conversion. My answer is always that such work is not my work at all. What I'm trying to do is to build people up. If they had not already received the light; if they had not already entered the path of regeneration, they would not be readers of *The Science of Thought Review*, for the simple reason that it is only those who have been spiritually awakened who can understand it.

Moreover, it is not sufficient for a person to pass through the experience known as conversion, for that is only the beginning of a very long journey. When the sick mind or soul has been healed, it is only convalescent. It has to be built up: it has to be integrated.

July 25

Life is a stream along which we are borne continuously. All remains well with us, so long as we keep to the middle of the stream, but unfortunately, we are prone to wander to the sides where we become caught up by various entanglements. We create our own disasters and sufferings through losing touch with our Divine centre. The troubles and disasters which we meet are love's way of bringing us back to our centre where alone we can experience peace and find true happiness.

July 26

When we start the regenerative life, a tremendous change takes place. It is like a school pupil being moved into a higher class, where they have to adapt to more exacting conditions. When we move upward spiritually, we have to become attuned to higher vibrations. Consequently, we find things difficult, simply because we fail to keep pace with the change which takes place in the spiritual tempo of our life.

The higher we rise and the farther we advance, the more is demanded of us. And this is why those who remain in the valley are not troubled. It also explains why those of us who aspire never seem to be given any rest, while other people can go comfortably on.

July 27

From time to time, I hear from depressed and low-spirited people, and while reading their letters, I feel that I want to make them laugh. I feel if only they could enjoy a good hearty laugh, they would soon get on top of their misery.

They would, however, at once reply to my exhortation: "But how can I laugh when my life is so bleak, and I am so miserable?" To which I should reply by asking: "But how can your life and circumstances be different from what they are so long as you remain so hopelessly depressed and low-spirited?"

July 28

Right thinking is true prayer. Instead of dwelling upon our difficulty or lack, we concentrate on the perfection of God's thought concerning us.

We declare the truth about God and humanity, for the truth about God is the real truth about us, created in the image and likeness of God. Humanity is spiritual, living always in the presence of God. All needs are supplied from before the foundation of the world.

The road is always open before us, for the Spirit goes before us preparing the way, and making smooth the path. We are guided by infinite wisdom... Whatever obstructs the path is removed, and whatever may be lacking is supplied. Already what is needed is on the way, and already what is obstructing is being removed. I thank Thee, Father, that this is so.

July 29

The remedy for that which happens in time is to raise the consciousness to that which is above time. This is what prayer does — or should do.

Prayer is not a matter of words, thoughts or ideas, but is rather a raising of the consciousness to a plane or realm which is above all words, thoughts and ideas. Many prayers are an attempt to bring God down to our human level. But true prayer is an attempt to raise our consciousness up to the Divine level.

Thus, we pass in consciousness from imperfection to perfection, from darkness to light.

July 30

In meditation we can realise, or allow our creative imagination to play round the idea, that we live and move and have our being in God: that we are surrounded by His infinite life, and that it interpenetrates our body, just as wireless waves pass into and through the strongest and stoutest of buildings.

We are immersed in God, as a fish is immersed in water. Just as water is the natural element of a fish, so also is God, the omnipresent Spirit, the natural element for us. We literally live, move and have our being in the one Spirit of Infinite Life. Its invisible rays of potent life pass into us and through us, and we are one with it.

At the same time, we can rest in the love of God, lean back on the everlasting arms and be at peace. This all makes for health and well-being.

July 31

Take God with you into this great experience. Directly you are willing to go with the experience, and when you realise that God is with you, and that therefore it does not matter what may happen to you, or what may become of you, for you are one with Him, you will enter into peace, and all fear will pass away.

You will know that God is love, that you can rest in the infinite love, that you can lean back on the everlasting arms, and they can never fail. You are one with that which changes not.

CHAPTER EIGHT

August

August 1

It follows that because reality is perfection to an infinite degree, the results of our prayers should be instantaneous, for the simple reason that there is nothing to be done. All that takes place is a change of consciousness. Instantaneous results are sometimes achieved, but more often outward results manifest gradually. This is because our consciousness is slow in changing. In some way, time interferes with our demonstration, but theoretically every result should be instantaneous, for the simple reason that, as Jesus said, when we know the truth, then the truth makes us free.

August 2

We have ears, but we hear not; we have eyes, but we see not. But prayer opens both our ears and our eyes. Over a long period of prayerful effort, we may not experience anything, then all at once something clicks and we "enter into the glorious liberty of the children of God". But even then, in spite of the fact that we have experienced an inward realisation, no outward change or deliverance may be seen. The thing to do is to keep on praising and thanking God for the deliverance which we know inwardly has taken place, but which has not yet manifested outwardly. This can hardly be described as an act of faith, for we actually know the truth which we have realised is the reality which alone is true. We therefore turn our attention from that which is false to that which alone is true and continue praising God for it.

August 3

We are to become members of a higher order than we can now imagine. There is as much difference between what we are now and what we are being trained to be as there is between a caterpillar and the glorious-winged creature which it finally becomes. Indeed, the difference is far greater — infinitely so.

If we set our affections on things above, then outward things fall into place. If, however, we concentrate upon things of this earth, we miss the mark and lose the heavenly vision.

August 4

The divine stillness which we experience in our contemplations is not stagnation or stasis, but is a state of infinitely harmonious motion. In the past I have spoken of reality as changeless. But that was liable to convey a wrong impression.

There is change in Heaven and joyous movement, but that is quite different from the change and decay which we experience on this plane. Instead of a change which goes down to decay and death, the change which takes place in the real world is joyous movement leading to ever-increasing beauty and joy.

August 5

Today, there come to some of us strange intimations of greater worlds and more wonderful lives. One reader writes to say that the Heavenly state is far more real to him than anything here. He adds that it is as if we are all clothed in heavy blankets, which, when we pass, we are glad to dispose of. But such awareness comes to us only after much travail.

I mention this for the encouragement of the many who are today passing through times of travail, and who may be wondering why.

The world stands at the crossroads. People, in their ignorance, are on the point of destroying themselves with their own inventions. It is those who **know** God alone who can save the world.

August 6

There are two kinds of people:

>   1. those who are maladjusted or disintegrated

2. those who are adjusted and integrated.

The former think that everyone else is wrong, and that therefore people and circumstances must be changed in order that they may be made happier. They want life to be adjusted to them, whereas what is needed is that they should become adjusted to life.

If our life is discordant and we are "in trouble", then what is needed is that we should become changed and not our circumstances. The adjustment needed has to be made by us.

August 7

If divine perfection is all around us and the essential goodness inherent in creation, then the imperfections of our life must be due to the fact that we are failing to express our true life-pattern.

If we want the divine pattern to appear in our life, we must surrender ourselves more completely to the Lord, the Christ within. If this is done, our outlook changes and we see with the eyes of Christ. That is to say, we see the divine perfection everywhere — in all people, in all circumstances, in all experiences.
Instead of demanding that life and others should be changed according to our pattern, we pray that we may be changed inwardly, in disposition and outlook, so that we out-picture the perfection of Christ.

August 8

The few who have endured and therefore attained to the higher state have only been a little more enduring than those who failed. A little more faithfulness, a little more endurance, a little more hanging on, so to speak, and then a wonderful transformation has taken place. All at once, those who have been persecuting them and trying to make their lives a misery have suddenly disappeared, almost magically, from the scene. It was all done with love, of course. The collapse of the persecution came when the victim loved their tormentors so much that they did not want them to go. Immediately that stage was reached, they disappeared, entirely of their own volition.

August 9

When we utter the word *Jesus*, we really utter the incommunicable name, which is unutterable because it stands for the ineffable. Consequently, even the most unlearned of us, and also the most sinful, can, by proxy so to speak, utter the name which is so holy as to be unutterable, even by archangels and the greatest of saints.

If we look at the sun, we find its light too powerful for us to endure, but we can look at a raindrop and see the sun reflected in it, without injury to our eyes.
Thus, there has been provided for us a way whereby we can invoke the Most High through repeating the name of Jesus.

August 10

When giving, we have to realise that actually we are not givers at all but are merely channels through which heavenly bounty flows. If we think that we are the givers, then we may impoverish ourselves by our giving.

If we think that we are doing the giving, and that what we are bestowing is our own bounty, then we are limited to the amount of our funds in hand or the amount that we can earn.

On the other hand, if we acknowledge that it is the bounty of Heaven that we are dispensing, and that we are merely a channel, then the supply will not fail, because it is an outpouring of infinite substance.

August 11

When we are at one with the Source, we do not need; we can only give. The things which formerly we desired, thinking that they were separate from us and that we lacked them, are now expressed by us, for we are one with *that* which forever *is*, and from whom all blessings flow. We are not *it* or *that*, in spite of what some teachings would have us believe, but one with it. And thus, we enter into our true home.

August 12

There are two stages in the life of faith. In the first, we seek for things and often enough get them. But then, we generally find they are not a complete solution of our problem. Also, the improvement may not prove permanent. Consequently, we have to keep on praying, first for one thing and then for another, and there may seem to be no end to it. This may last for years, and of course it is a good stage at the time.

In due course, this brings the aspirant to the crisis, in which they surrender all to God, after which they desire only to do the will of God, and for the Divine Spirit or Christ to work through them, using them as a channel.

Seeking God's kingdom and His righteousness first leads to a permanent state of well-being. Instead of having to treat or pray, first for this thing and then for that, we abide constantly in the consciousness of divine good.

August 13

Most people feel that they stand in need of divine blessings. These can be secured, not by seeking them, but by entering into a higher consciousness. In this higher consciousness there exists, as eternal realities, all manner of divine good and every possible harmony and satisfaction. Consequently, when we have entered into this higher consciousness, we find that all things are ours and always have been. We find also that we reach that plane where evil never happened.

August 14

Again and again, the thought may come to us that we are trying to find the Great Stillness in order to solve our problem or overcome the difficulty confronting us. This has to be rejected, for we have to learn to "stand still, and see the salvation of the Lord". It is not we who are doing anything. We become still, and yet more still, until at last we become absorbed in the Divine order, and entirely at one with the will of God, which of course is perfect — perfect for us and perfect for everyone else.

Also, it is when we no longer want things to be altered that a condition is brought about which makes a divine adjustment possible.

August 15

In seeking the kingdom of God, which is a state of high consciousness, we have to become very positive-minded indeed. Aspiring Godwards, we rise higher and higher in consciousness until at last we enter into the *great stillness* or *silence*, which is the presence of God realised.

Sinking down into a state of negative passiveness should never be indulged in.

It is necessary that we should be positive-minded at all times and that we should be open only to the divine or Holy Spirit of truth. If we are in any doubt, we should keep on repeating the name of Jesus, or Jesus Christ, until we realise His presence.

August 16

My experience has convinced me that we could succeed and accomplish everything perfectly if we would only get ourselves out of the way, so to speak. Perfection is always present, but we distort it so that imperfection is manifested instead. We do not have to create perfection, but only to release it. I believe that there will come a time when humanity will live and work by releasing the hidden perfection, and have access to all knowledge by intuition. But this will not come about in my time.

August 17

Time and space, we are told, are merely limitations of consciousness. They are infinity, imperfectly perceived. It is the same with our lacks and limitations: they are wholeness, imperfectly perceived. The reality is infinite perfection — that is, perfection that is infinite. Consequently, our prayers are answered before we can ask them. They are already answered before we even begin to pray. "Before they pray, I will answer, and while they are yet speaking, I will hear."

August 18

Praying without ceasing, as taught by the Greek and Russian Orthodox Churches, is not practised really to persuade God to do anything, but rather to bring the mind of the one who prays into conformity with the Divine Mind. What the neophyte prays for is already accomplished, but their constant praying changes their consciousness so that they can realise it.

August 19

To beginners, affirmative prayer which declares that what they feel they need is already accomplished may seem like telling lies to themselves, for obviously what they declare to be true in an inward sense is not true in an outward sense. When this is the case, I think that "asking" prayer should be continued with, until some measure of inward understanding has been reached. It must be emphasised that what one declares to be true is only true in an interior sense. It is not true in any exterior sense, because the outer life is not a presentation of truth, but only a travesty of it.

Each one should pray in that way which is suitable for them at the time, and which suits their stage of understanding. If they use a form of prayer that is too advanced, they will probably end in confusion.

August 20

People often ask: why should calamities come upon humankind? If God is good, why does He allow such things to come to pass? If there is a Power that is friendly to people, why does it not act on their behalf? The answer is that humankind ignores the Infinite Power and Intelligence, and lives outside the Divine order; consequently, they are subject to disorder.

If we would live Divinely guided lives, we must, of course, make contact with, and become attuned to, our Divine Source — the Infinite Intelligence which we call God.

August 21

We are forgiven our trespasses to the extent that we are willing to forgive "them that trespass against us". By forgiving others, we make it possible that we should be forgiven. Actually, we are always forgiven, for there never is a time when Divine Love does not forgive, but we cannot enter into God's forgiveness until we have freely forgiven those who have wronged us.

This is also the reason why those who drop their resentments and freely forgive those who have wronged them become healed of the disease which the hatred has produced. Through forgiving and loving their enemies, and praying they may be blessed in every possible way, they become raised into a state of union with the Lord of Love, who is perfect life, health, wholeness and joy.

August 22

Those who are surrendered to the Lord of Love, and who try to be love itself in all their relations with others, will be filled with exquisite joy when the love vibrations that are continually being poured out upon this earth become more intense. Also, the blessedness of their life will be increased. But, let me repeat, it is only those who are attuned who will be able to face infinite love and purity.

August 23

When we turn to God, desiring only that the will of the One, the Whole, be done in us and in our life, we take the first step in the path of liberation. Until we enter into "the liberty of the children of God", we are in prison. This cannot be accomplished by praying for things, or for our life to be made easier, or that others should act differently towards us. Our prayer should therefore be that of the model prayer given by Jesus: "Thy kingdom (a state of perfect order and harmony) come: Thy will be done, on earth (in our life) as it is in Heaven (that realm where infinite wisdom and love have unimpeded action)." When we pray in this fashion, we pray in harmony with the highest wisdom. We come into harmony with the current of the universe.

August 24

It is difficult to live the life of love — the love which is the love of Christ. If we claim to be love, to be a follower of the Lord of Love, we find it so difficult to do the dangerous thing, to act as love would have us act, leaving the future with God. It may seem to be the utmost folly and improvidence, to do as love prompts us to do. But if we respond to love's impulse — we are not forced to do so by any means — we find that underneath us are the everlasting arms, and that these never fail. We find that if we act as love prompts us to act, greater liberty and freedom become ours.

August 25

Our disciplines may be sharp, but they are sharp because it is necessary for our highest good that they should be sharp. If we co-operated with life more than we do, and if we disciplined ourselves more, then the discipline that is forced upon us from life would be unnecessary — or at any rate less necessary — so that it would not come to us except in a modified form.

August 26

It is as though we heard the indwelling Lord saying:

> "My son, my daughter, give me thy heart. Yield all to me, so that I can protect you and keep you in

quietness and confidence. Yield all to me, so that my strength [which is infinite] may become your strength. Some of the experiences through which I shall lead you may not be to your liking, but if you will trust me, I will lead you through them victoriously; and in them all you will find me. If you trust me fully, no evil will ever be able to come nigh you. If you trust me fully, the only experiences that can come to you will be those that are prepared by my love and wisdom to bring you to your eternal joy."

August 27

I have known people who have sought healing for years, in vain, who have been healed when they left off praying for healing and have rejoiced in the Lord instead. Through waiting upon God, they have received such a lovely realisation of His presence and love that they have said: "I don't want to be healed if to be healed should mean losing this lovely sense of God's presence and love. I want this presence, no matter what the loss may be." Then, because they had chosen the better part, and because they had put the kingdom first, before self, and because they let God come into their life through their surrender, they were healed.

August 28

We can do no good for others if we starve our own soul and neglect our inner life. We cannot feed the hungry if we are weakened through lack of communion with God. We cannot help others if we possess not that spiritual power which comes only through quiet waiting upon God in the secret place.

We can do the best work, in the best way, only if we wait upon God to keep alive that spiritual part of us that is filled with wisdom and power. Through this, our life proceeds along definite lines of progress. Like a plant, our inward spiritual life grows from day to day.

August 29

Not only does the natural person think that they are separate from God, but they also think that they are separated from their fellows. Yet this is not the case. Just as islands are joined together under the sea through the medium of Mother Earth, so are people united in the common parenthood of God. By hurting a fellow creature, a person hurts themselves. Every cruel word, every selfish deed, every untrue implication in which someone indulges, recoils upon themselves. In the same manner, every act and thought of love blesses the one who sends as much as it blesses the one who receives. When humankind as a whole realises this truth, wars and cruelties will cease.

August 30

The true art of life is in living our life as nearly as possible in accordance with the dictates of the higher wisdom. We may often fall short of the Divine Ideal, but if we persevere, never giving up — although perhaps at times discouraged — we are bound to win through. When we endeavour to live such a life, we have the whole power of the universe at our back, for we are in harmony with the purpose of life.

August 31

As we move forward towards the ineffable, we lay aside all names and forms; we also emerge beyond all thoughts and ideas about God. Consequently, because we cease trying to limit the limitless, it begins to become possible for us to go forward. All forms, thoughts, names and ideas have to be laid aside by us. So, as they arise, we gently brush them aside and continue steadily forward to *that* which transcends all forms, thoughts, names and ideas.
And so we move forward to the nameless, ineffable one. We discard everything until at last we come to nothing...and when we have come to nothing — we find that we have found everything.

Chapter Nine

September

September 1

There are times when no text or passage of scripture appeals to us. Everything may seem to be dead and lifeless, and also, we ourselves may seem to have lost all power of spiritual perception. When this is so, we should browse over the scriptures with a receptive mind, with our soul open to Divine influences. For a time, this may be fruitless, and then suddenly a text or passage may spring into life and radiate light and understanding. Then it is that we understand what Jesus meant when He said: "Ye shall know the truth, and the truth shall make you free."

September 2

Although the real object of raising the consciousness is that we may reach a state of Divine union, yet at first the neophyte has to be satisfied with something less. They should not be discouraged because they cannot raise their consciousness to supernal heights, for everything is right at the time. A rosebud is not a rose, but it will become one in due time. It must not be impatient, nor must it sigh or feel discouraged or inferior, for in due course it will unfold effortlessly and harmoniously, until it becomes a perfect rose, enchanting the eye and spreading its fragrance everywhere.

September 3

The more we fight our negative experiences, the worse they appear, or the more completely defeated we become. This is because we are trying to fight evil on its own plane where it is all-powerful and undefeatable. But, when we raise our consciousness to a higher level, we raise our problem or trouble to that plane where it never happened, and where evil has no power. This is why Jesus said: "Resist not evil," and "Agree with thine adversary." Instead of fighting and resisting, we raise the whole trouble to that plane where harmony and order reign, and disharmony and disorder are, of course, quite unknown.

September 4

By raising your consciousness, even though it be ever so little, you become joined up with the supreme consciousness. When you refuse to entertain negative thoughts of failure and defeat, and instead think thoughts of overcoming and victory through the power within and through your inherent oneness with the one infinite life, then, although your attempts may appear to you very crude, you will have raised your consciousness above the plane where things and events can hurt you, or really hinder you.

September 5

We can become more in tune with life, and enter into harmony with our environment, by loving and blessing all our fellows, all animals, all creation, in fact. We can spend a few minutes every day in blessing all our environment, and in sending our benedictions of love and compassion to the whole universe. If we practise this, instead of merely reading about it, we not only enter into a harmonious fellowship with the whole, but we also see God everywhere. And, if we are able to see God everywhere, it is because God indwells us, for it is only with His eyes that we see. In one sense, God can only see Himself reflected, so to speak, in His creation. If, therefore, God indwells us, we see God everywhere.

September 6

The truth is hidden in all myths and fairy tales. A prince leaves home and is put under a spell, so that he appears as something or somebody quite different. At last, the spell is broken, and he finds himself again a prince. In fact, he has been a prince (son of his father the king) all the time, but the spell has made him forget his true identity and to appear unlike, and behave as something unlike, his true self.

In like manner, we have left our Father's home. We have gone into an alien land. We too have come under the spell of this world and appear to be, and also behave as, a stranger in a foreign land. But then comes the time of awakening. It is revealed to us who and what we truly are, and we say, like the prodigal son: "I will arise and go to my Father."

September 7

The method of concentrating upon a divine promise, instead of trying to destroy our trouble, accomplishes detachment and enables us to make a motion towards God. After which, union with the divine follows. We have to make a motion or movement of faith, in the same way that the woman pressed forward, detaching herself from the crowd, and touched the hem of Jesus' robe.

September 8

If we think heavenly thoughts, then we become attached to heavenly powers and potencies, and also heavenly beings are drawn to us, who seek to raise us up to their own level. If, however, we allow ourselves to entertain thoughts of weakness, self-pity, fear, or failure, then we become attached to harmful influences that seek to drag us down to their own level. We cannot serve two masters, even as Jesus said. It is a glorious thing to know that if we train our mind to think heavenly thoughts, we are ministered to by heavenly agencies and upheld by heavenly powers.

September 9

If we sigh for better opportunities and greater powers and abilities, and especially if we envy other people and engage in self-pity, then we shut the door upon all possibilities of progress and overcoming. But if we start where we are, and make the best use of what we have, then nothing can stay our upward climb.

Consequently, we do not pray for easier lives, but rather that we should be stronger people. We do not pray for greater opportunities, but only that we may make the best use of those we already have. It does not matter how low down we may be, we can rise to unbelievable heights, if we make a start now, and keep on keeping on.

September 10

Jesus found it necessary to withdraw from the press of crowds and the demands of thousands of clamouring people, in order to "rest awhile", and also to pray to His Father. Such prayer is like putting an electric accumulator "on charge". During our intercourse with the world, we become depleted and exhausted, like a rundown accumulator. When, however, we wait upon God and stay our mind upon Him, spiritual currents flow into us until we are refilled with divine power.

September 11

As nothing has to be done really, but only our eyes opened to the perfection which is already present everywhere, it follows we do not have to wrestle with God or strain or struggle in order that what we want should be achieved. Instead, all that we have to do is to pray that our eyes may be opened, so that we can see the Divine perfection which is all around us.

Instead of "Lord, send us protection", or "Lord, change so and so", what we need to do is to pray, "Lord, open Thou mine eyes that I may see Thy protection", or "the truth concerning so and so". Let me see Thy salvation (Divine wholeness and perfection – the Divine idea) which Thou hast prepared for me before the foundation of the world – the eternal truth, without beginning or end, which was, and is, and evermore shall be.

September 12

We can never explain with the intellect things which are beyond the intellect. In order to know, we have to be. That is to say: if we are to know a certain thing, we must become the thing we seek to know. For instance, if we would know love, we must ourselves become love. Also, we can know God only to the extent that we become Godlike.

September 13

The breathing of the Spirit is deep and rhythmic: it conforms to the breathing note of the spiritual universe; it keeps time, so to speak, with the pulsations of the universal life. Because of this it forms an important part in our regeneration.

The extended consciousness brings the power of the eternal to us so that we partake of it and enter into it. Through being conscious of infinite life being present, and extending in consciousness beyond the range of our ordinary breath, we are able to breathe in an extended way, to include the life eternal, so that each breath brings into our being the spiritual reality, so that our inner life is nourished. But it must not be forced or sought after. It must come of itself as a result of dwelling upon or contemplating divine or heavenly things.

September 14

Cultivating the exalted consciousness which raises us above the cares and fret of life is helpful in the extreme, and vitally necessary, yet it is really in the practical affairs of life that we attain. Life brings to us the very experience that we need. It is generally the one thing in the world that we do not want to meet. It touches us on the raw; it attacks our weak spot; it makes us wonder what is going to happen next or where life is going to lead us. But through the experience we may become strong in the quality that we lack, wise in the understanding we need, and through it all find God in a new and intimate sense, such as we have never known before.

We advance along two paths simultaneously – the mystical and the practical.

September 15

If we think of ourselves as sons in ourselves, or gods in our own right, then we become estranged from divine grace. If we continue so to regard ourselves, then after a time – it may be years – we meet with the experiences which those who would be gods must meet; and then all we have built up is dashed to pieces because God is not in us.

Jesus illustrated this in the allegory of the man who built his house upon the sand:

> *"And the rain descended, and the floods came, and the winds blew, and beat upon that house: and it fell: and great was the fall thereof."*

September 16

Our difficult task is always just to venture a little farther than we have ever gone before, in love, forbearance, trust, service and self-sacrifice. We know that our Lord went much further, without any limit or reservation at all; and we also know that thousands of others have gone much farther than we.

We say that our experience is more than flesh and blood can bear. This is true, but in our true selves, as sons of God, we are spiritual beings: and therefore, able to bear what is too much for flesh and blood. If, therefore, we make a venture of faith and go a little farther than we feel we can go, we find that God *"is able to do exceedingly abundantly, above all we can ask or think, according to the power that works in us."*

September 17

Give thanks, O my soul, that there is nothing but God (good), and that God is infinite love.
Give thanks that there is no disharmony in the divine mind, but only perfect harmony and peace.
Give thanks that there is no darkness, but only the light of light.

September 18

When we approach the spiritual and eternal, we can only pray that the will of the highest may be done. The prayer of self-will seeks only for a smaller good – what the finite mind thinks is good – but the prayer to the eternal and highest is for the larger good, i.e. that which is in harmony with the will and purpose of the highest heaven.

September 19

The prayer of the heart is a turning of the heart to God in love and devotion. Of course we have to use words at first. Indeed, we may be so beset with troubles and bewilderments that we feel we must tell God all about them. Also, we may have to declare the perfection of God and the Divine order, to cleanse our mind of error and misunderstanding.

Jesus said of those who crucified Him: *"Father, forgive them for they know not what they do."* Their minds were full of misunderstanding, and so are our minds, and the way to cleanse them of error is to pray.

September 20

The highest form of prayer is to become silent and still before God. Such prayer is wordless, but not everyone is ready to practise the wordless prayer. We are led up to it by stages. Firstly, our prayers may be selfish and self-centred. Next, they may be more universal and cosmic. Finally, we realise that there is really nothing to pray for, and that all we need is God.

When praying for things we are making use of effort. But when we commune with God, we simply rest in Him and are carried along effortlessly, as it were, on the bosom of a mighty river of peace.

September 21

As I gaze at the flowers on my desk, and listen in imagination to their silvery voices, I know that love can never forsake me. *"Look on us,"* they seem to say, *"we are expressions of the love that never grows cold, of that bounty and mercy that never fail. We come to express to you the Father's love. We come from the unknown and the invisible to tell you that all is well – that beauty and joy, and bounteous plenty are the Divine intention towards humankind. The one who provides such profusion can never fail to supply your every need, or to keep you amid all the vicissitudes of your life."*

September 22

Some readers find it difficult to realise that all that is required in their lives is a divine adjustment. Others may recognise this truth but are afraid to pray for a divine adjustment. They fear what God might do, if they were to leave the choice to Him. To do so would be equivalent to praying that the will of God should be done. They would never dream of praying that God's will should be done, for fear of what He might do to them if they were to do so.

But of course, God is infinite wisdom and infinite love. Therefore, the divine will is definitely wise, and also is infinite love in expression. Consequently, we can pray no better prayer than that the divine will should be done.

September 23

So many feel they have so many supplications to make that they have no time for the Silence, or to realise that God is bringing about a divine adjustment. Consequently, they miss the mark. The Lord says to us: *"Be still and know that I am God."* It is when we become perfectly still, in God, that the action of God takes place. And the effortless action of God is what produces a divine adjustment.

September 24

There is an interior and perfect rhythm which might be described as God's activity, and this, of course, is perfect harmony. So long as this rhythm remains undisturbed and unbroken all is well with us, and we are filled with peace and joy.

When we lose it, the object of prayer is to bring about a restoration. If we pray for things, we simply play about excitedly on the surface; whereas if we become perfectly quiet in God, we enter into a deep peace – the peace which God Himself enjoys. We breathe rhythmically in tune with the hidden life of God.

September 25

If there were more contemplatives than there are, then the world would be saved. By contemplatives is meant those who have found God through meditation and the Silence and are able to contemplate the essential goodness.

When we truly pray to God, we make a direct approach. When we enter the true silence, we also make a direct approach: we actually experience God. Again, when we truly meditate, we make a direct approach to God. In meditation we cast aside all thoughts and ideas that are not of God, until only God remains.

September 26

In order to set out on our search for God, we have first to surrender ourselves entirely to Him, desiring that He should do whatever may be best for us, having in view the ultimate goal of the union of the soul with its divine source. After such surrender, all the experiences which come to us are designed to bring us nearer to the heart of God. Some experiences may not be to our liking, while others may be hard to bear, but each one tends to change us back into the divine likeness from which we have wandered.

September 27

In our meditation, we can form a picture of a world similar to this present world, but with all its disorders removed; where everything is done for love's sake, where everyone cooperates with everyone else, and where everything comes to pass at the right time, in a perfectly harmonious manner. This is the reverse of daydreaming, for it is positive and constructive. We fix our attention upon the eternal goodness. We persevere in doing this until we feel what we are picturing.

September 28

The object of prayer should be an endeavour to see the disturbing circumstance as it is in God, instead of as it appears to the senses. All disorder is a departure from the perfect order, which is the reality. Prayer or meditation is therefore an attempt on our part to find and know truth – that perfect harmony in which we realise that *"all is well, a thousand times well, both now and a million years hence."*

September 29

Most of us have to learn through experience. We find ourselves confronted by difficulties and obstacles so great that it seems impossible for us to move. We appear to be completely shut in and brought to a standstill. The thing to do then is to attempt the most difficult and seemingly impossible thing – to go forward, putting our whole trust in God. Then we find the way is really open before us, and that it has never been closed.

September 30

We can change our thoughts and minds, even as Jesus said. Indeed, in the course of time, we become so transformed that we no longer respond to thoughts of a wrong type; consequently, they are unconsciously deflected. The acceptance of good thoughts becomes habitual. It is just as natural for us to accept good thoughts as at one time it was natural for us to attract and accept evil thoughts.

Chapter Ten

October

October 1

Our work is not the healing or curing of diseases of the body, but rather their prevention through the finding of God's inward peace and the joy of His salvation. We cannot even begin to find God's inward peace until we have forgiven to the uttermost.

Of course, we cannot transmit God's inward peace to others if we do not possess it ourselves. So, our duty must always be to be so filled with God's peace that others become conscious of it. This is possible to the extent that we wait upon the Lord and enter into "the glorious liberty of the children of God".

October 2

How can we raise our consciousness to the plane of reality in which is complete fullness and adequate sufficiency? We think about God and His completeness until we get beyond thought and enter into a realisation of that which is beyond human thought and know that we actually are the thing or state realised. Such thinking about God and His completeness is real prayer. It leads to realisation in which we know the truth of reality by direct cognition.

October 3

Truth statements are helpful if we declare them, even if we do not understand their full import. There are thousands of people today who are making use of statements which are true only of reality (divine perfection). If they were to think they were true of the self they would simply be telling lies to themselves, about themselves.

Such statements are true of the divine perfection, but not of the "self". They are, however, true of the real spiritual person (our real self), *"who is born not of blood, nor of the will of the flesh, nor of the will of man, but God."*

October 4

The majority of people want their circumstances altered first, after which they will change their thoughts. *If only my circumstances were different*, they will say, *I could get along very well.* They may also say: *"It is easy for you to think rightly. I wonder what you would do if your life was as full of difficulties as mine?"* They do not realise that our better circumstances may be the result of better thinking, or that their difficult conditions may possibly be partly due to their own wrong thinking and emotional reactions.

October 5

Those who live by faith, generally speaking, work harder than ordinary people. But they do not work in order to earn a living. Their supply comes from God. Their work is done as an act of service to the world, to others, and to God, without any thought of reward. Consequently, it is of a higher and better quality.

October 6

What is popularly understood as happiness generally implies a certain amount of self-centredness. If all goes well with us, if we win some of life's prizes, and if we become the object of praise and adulation, then we may think we are happy. But it is not real happiness, for if we lose our popularity, we become miserable.

Those who are unawakened are forever seeking happiness, but of course they never find it. Real happiness, if ever it does come to us, comes only when we do not seek it. It is one of the "things added".

October 7

A person with a mission is above what is ordinarily regarded as happiness. They do not think of it. All they want to do is to get on with the work they have come to do. They are driven forward by a consuming passion to prosecute their life's work. Let others think about happiness ...

Although probably unaware of the fact, each aspiring soul is here on a mission. There is a divine purpose behind each experience: a divine pattern underlying each life. The will of God is always working on our behalf, in order to enable us to reach our goal of union with the divine.

October 8

One who responds to the call becomes one of the chosen. After giving their life to God they enter upon a severe training. They are tested and tried, as others are not. Often, they are brought to the brink of despair. Then it is that they make a fresh dedication and yield up their all again to God. Each experience brings about the apparent death of "self". But the self is a hydra-headed monster that refuses to die, and new heads grow in the place of the one cut off. However, the final result of a lifetime of surrenders to the will of God, and rededications of life to Him, must and do result in complete union.

October 9

It is the law of life that *"one man should die for the people"*. That is, those who are strong should bear the infirmities of the weak, and also suffer many things (giving up their life again and again) in order that others should go free.

October 10

Many people miss the mark through trying to save their life instead of losing it. They cling to the "self" life of two-ness or duality and resist the experiences that come to them and which, if accepted, would bring them into a state of oneness with the divine.

When remedial or disciplinary experiences come, they try to "wipe them out" by prayer or metaphysical treatments. Instead of agreeing with the adversary in the way Jesus taught, they resist him. The consequence being that they make no progress, but rather hinder themselves through making use of potent powers of the spirit in order to destroy the very thing which would, if accepted, have raised them up to the very heart of God.

October 11

John says in the 2nd chapter of his 1st epistle: *"Whosoever is born of God doth not commit sin; for his seed remaineth in him: and he cannot sin, because he is born of God."* It is the true inward spiritual person who is born of God. The outward, visible person sins and perishes, but the inward, true, spiritual person *"doeth the will of God (and) abideth forever."*

October 12

The aspirant cannot enter into divine union without preparation. They have to pass through what is termed the stripping stage. They have to be stripped of everything that is unlike God; for it is obvious that nothing that is unlike the mind of God can enter the mind of God. And so we surrender, first this thing, and then that desire, together with all the worldly ambitions and pride. All selfishness, all fears, and all that the "self" implies, and also all our ideas about God, have to be surrendered: for we can never know God by knowing things about God, or by entertaining theories concerning God.

October 13

But, possessing a desire to know God ... is not enough. We have to set out on a search for God. We cannot attain to a state of union through meditation or contemplation alone. Neither can we find God through mind or intellectual strivings only. No, we have to go on a journey.

The journey is packed with experiences of a most searching character. Those who cherish the idea that attainment to a state of union is possible without tears are due to meet with a rude awakening.

October 14

The mystical pathway is one of repeated surrenders to the divine will. Again and again, we come to the end of our own resources, so that we can but cast ourselves upon God, who is our final resource. When all else fails, still God remains.

October 15

Those who are still in the valley, satisfied with lowly things, will one day become filled with a compelling urge to climb the spiritual mountain and stand in the divine light and radiance and glory. At present they cannot understand those who do such things as climb mountains, or endure dark nights of the soul, or fight battles with their Apollyons. They think everyone should be happy and comfortable.

But the day will come when the bovine stage will no longer satisfy, and in its place will be born in them a desire to explore the heights, to breathe a rare atmosphere, and also to obtain a wider view.

October 16

Arranging one's life in an orderly fashion can never give any real inward satisfaction. I have met "self-made" people and they all agree that they were far happier when they were poor. Getting on in life was "fun" while they were still striving, but arriving at the top of the tree, they became bored and miserable. Satisfaction can only be found in the struggle upwards, and that satisfaction is something greater than mere happiness.

October 17

The Lord looks after His own if only we will let Him; that is, if we do not prevent His bounty from manifesting through lack of faith. The supply that comes through wrestling with the world by our own efforts is hard to obtain and difficult to hold. But the supply that comes from the Lord comes softly and gently like a fall of snow in the night-time and is held easily, for no one will seek to take it away.

October 18

The name which can be uttered is not the unutterable name. Directly we give God a name, we bring Him down to our own level, so to speak. God is beyond all names and all definitions: beyond all praise and our highest worship: He is beyond, beyond our highest conceptions of God: beyond our highest flights of imagination.

Because of this, we are told that those who wait upon the Lord shall renew their strength. Waiting on the Lord means staying our mind in a worshipful way upon that which is beyond our highest conception of life.

October 19

As we advance in our worship and adoration, we lay aside first this idea and then that, also all theories about God, and all attempts to explain God. Until at last we get beyond the human mind and come to nothing, which of course is beyond everything conceivable by the human intellect. Consequently, when we have reached this stage, we discover that we have found everything, or rather, that which is beyond everything.

October 20

This is the life upon which we can draw – the life which is beyond life. This is why our text says that it is *"they that wait upon the Lord (God in His transcendence) who shall renew their strength"*, not those who wait upon the Lord (God brought down within the limitations of human thought).

October 21

There is no need to implore God to do anything, or to change anything, for all His ways are perfect. Therefore, all that we need to do is to wait upon God, and become perfectly quiet before Him, putting aside all ideas and thoughts and desires, and also quietening our wild imagination, until at last our mind begins to vibrate in correspondence with the mind of God, and thus we find His inward peace.

As soon as we are brought into harmonious relationship with God – that is, directly we vibrate in correspondence with the mind of God – then a divine adjustment follows.

October 22

We ourselves cannot enter the heavenly consciousness. We have to become changed from glory to glory, even as by the Spirit of the Lord. When we are like heaven we can enter heaven; when we have heaven within us, we can enter a heavenly consciousness. When we are ready for it, and not before, the consciousness begins to expand, until it becomes immense and vast, and this is accompanied by a consciousness of tremendous power, and an understanding that is as deep as the universe and which embraces eternity.

October 23

I have seen some who must have been near to attaining the stage of translation, for their faces shone with heavenly light, and there was a brightness and shining clearness about them which made ordinary people appear dull and muddy by comparison. This would not be apparent to an ordinary observer, for it takes a saint to see a saint, which means, of course, that one can recognise spirituality in others only to the extent of one's own spirituality.

October 24

We should spend more time in prayer, meditation and contemplation. We need to turn to the Lord more often than we do. This does not mean that we have to be advanced practitioners in the art of prayer. All that we need to do is to pray according to our present light and understanding. The essential thing is that our prayer should be sincere and from the heart. Praise and thanksgiving are also most helpful. Inward prayer of praise and thanksgiving can be practised until it becomes continuous and self-motivated so that it proceeds day and night – a ceaseless stream of praise and adoration.

October 25

The way of heaven is different from the way of the world. It strives in neither direction but is sure in all its action. Human beings strive either from one extreme or the other. The ordinary life is one of contending powers and opposing forces. But the sage does not contend or oppose: he remains at the midpoint, or point of balance, where all opposing forces are reconciled. He is then *"sure in all his actions"*, for instead of strife and struggle the silent, instantaneous action of God takes place.

October 26

The net of love is not only vast: it is also widely meshed. This net of love, because its mesh is so wide, allows us plenty of free will. We may go our own self-willed way as much as we like, and through so doing may create for ourselves much suffering; but love is there all the time, and when we have spent ourselves and have repented of our folly, we find that the mesh of love is there to prevent us from being lost. And what is true of us is true of all, for *"naught from it is ever lost"*.

October 27

There will be no strain so long as we keep up with life and continue marching towards the hills of God. Everything comes to pass by reason of its own spontaneity. While, apparently, we are engaged in action, yet we are not the actor. While it is true that in one sense, we have to be active, go forward and keep up with life, yet actually, in a real sense, God is the only doer, and He it is who brings all things to pass.

October 28

Through a continual turning to the Lord, contemplating His divine perfection, there takes place in us what is termed a *"systematic and orderly unfoldment of the Gnostic faculties of the soul, without which knowledge of reality is impossible."* This is what I have always described as an inward spiritual faculty of direct knowing by the soul, which discerns truth through intuition and not through the intellect.

October 29

No one can ever destroy the unity of the whole. This understanding or realisation does not come through head learning, but through quiet contemplation in a spirit of devotion and praise.

October 30

The way or path that we are endeavouring to teach, i.e., the way of contemplation, devotion, love and union, is a pathway of blessedness.

It is a pathway of joy leading to bliss indescribable. Every time that we turn to the Lord and contemplate His divine perfections, and enter into His peace, we not only tend to become changed into His likeness, but our pathway becomes smoothed, the circumstances of our lives adjusted and our problems solved.

October 31

If we look upon life as a stream, we see that if we keep in the middle of the current all will be well with us. But if we wander off to the sides, then we collide with the banks, or get caught up in snags, or sucked away into eddies, all of which cause us difficulty and suffering in addition to hindering our progress. The remedy for all this is not to worry about or fight against the obstacles along the banks, but to keep to the middle of the stream.

CHAPTER ELEVEN

November

November 1

By nature of our thoughts, we bring into action forces and happenings which are beyond our power to control. If we think heavenly thoughts, we become linked up with heavenly power and potency, which work on our behalf and for our good. They do for us "exceeding abundantly, above all that we can ask or think". Positive thought or true prayer switches on the power which creates beauty, harmony, order, and all manner of divine good. And this process continues, even while we sleep.

November 2

Instead of struggling and striving, we accept the fullness of blessing which God is always wanting to bestow. It is not a matter of striving to get, but a willingness to accept and pass on that which we receive. We do not cling to, or hoard what comes to us, but pass it on, thus keeping it circulating. This is as necessary to the well-being of our economy as the circulation of the blood is to the well-being of our body.

November 3

If our own individual world becomes transformed, and our associates changed for the better through an integrating change in ourselves, then because this change takes place in us and our own little world, it follows that in course of time the whole world, together with all its people, will become changed in the same way.

November 4

Some have been literally pushed out of the life we were leading and had the door slammed either in our face, or on our backs: and we found we could simply do nothing about it. Then it was that we found another door opening. And passing through the open door we found ourselves in our right place, and also doing our right work. That is, the work which we had come here to do. Then it was that we realised that all the experiences through which we had come were but a preparation for the new sphere of service upon which we had just entered.

November 5

Every difficulty, trial and disappointment is designed by infinite wisdom and infinite love to bring you a step nearer to the glorious consummation of all your hopes and highest aspirations. Only keep your attention fixed on God, the beautiful, the good and the true. Do not dwell on your failures. Above all, remember and practise the advice of the wise Emerson: *"Do not bark against the bad, but chant the beauties of the good."*

November 6

When giving, we have to realise that we're not giving at all but are merely being used as a channel by the one infinite, inexhaustible source – God. If we think that it is we who are giving, out of our own limited resources, then we may soon find our pocket empty. In effect, we cut ourselves off from the creative divine supply. If, however, we realise that it is the inexhaustible supply that is being drawn upon, we find that in some mysterious way we're not impoverished by our giving, and that the demands that are made upon us are met without effort.

November 7

Every time we think of war, we can rise above the pairs of opposites and realise that which is above good and evil, and peace and war – the love which in due course will overcome all violence by reconciling everything to itself. Whenever the thought comes to us of limitation, we can raise our consciousness to that fullness of life which can never grow less. Whenever we think of mortality and death, we can rise above them and realise our oneness with the one perfect life which knows no decay and which is always self-renewing from within itself, and which is as potent today as millions of years ago.

November 8

When we turn to the one supreme Lord all the divine forces hasten to minister to us. When we turn to the one omnipotent power great spiritual potencies are set in motion to work on our behalf. Day by day these divine powers and potencies work for good and also carry on their activities while we are asleep.

Consequently, we are not alone in our efforts and struggles God-wards. We are upheld by powers of light.

November 9

The divine momentum gathers strength with the years. Also, every time that we turn to the Lord something is added to it. Every true desire, every noble thought, every selfless action, also adds something to this divine momentum, which leaves sin and failure behind and pushes us along to our highest good and our greatest joy.

November 10

The burning bush again becomes a reality. Everything is ablaze with God. God, indeed, is everywhere. The glory of God shines through simple things, and around us is the radiance of heaven.

It is not only in animate things that God is being seen, nor in the majestic movement of sun and stars, but also in inanimate things such as stones and clods of earth. Every stone and clod is filled with God's glory. A stone is filled with eternal energy; it is luminous with celestial fire.

November 11

When we enter into the inner kingdom we breathe deeply, rhythmically and without effort in correspondence with the harmony and rhythm of the spirit – we are attuned to the life of God. Our soul breathes the very life of God, which knows no disease and suffers from no decay.

Our soul breathes the life which is perfect, pure and lovely. We find ourselves at one with that life which is manifest in millions of different ways, but with infinite order, coordination and perfection.

November 12

If we keep on turning to our divine source, then we shall be kept in tune. Even if we do but keep saying: *"I thank Thee, I thank Thee, I thank Thee"*, it will keep us in touch. Also, as we do our daily tasks we can keep in touch with our centre. We can, as it were, do our work with one hand, while with the other we touch the feet of the Lord.

November 13

When we become still, we may find that this is not sufficient. We may find that we have to enter into an even greater, deeper and more effective state of stillness. And this may have to be repeated, so that we go deeper and deeper, until at last we penetrate the very secret, inner essence of the life of God. When this takes place, we are, as Jacob Boehme said, that which God was before our false and wayward imagination arose.

November 14

Our true life is really like the graceful flight of a bird, or the dancing of insects in the sunlight. Instead of being dull and heavy, we should be light, like a bird on the wing, or thistledown borne on the gentle breeze. We are far too serious. I firmly believe that there is laughter in heaven – a joyous expression of infinite joy.

November 15

We live in a perfect universe. What we have to do is to discover it, not to alter it, or try to improve it. Jesus made manifest the divine perfection when He healed diseased people. But He healed at different levels, according to the understanding of those who came to Him. At the highest level He said: *"Go thy way: thy son liveth."* At a lower level He made clay of spittle and anointed a blind man's eyes. But in each case, perfection was already present.

What Jesus did was to reveal the ever-present perfect wholeness to their respective understandings.

November 16

When we are confronted with some disturbing experience, instead of meeting it with resentment, or being overcome by fear, or upset by giving way to annoyance, we inwardly realise our oneness with the Lord, instantly becoming composed, poised, balanced, and at peace with all people. Then we hold up the trouble for divine guidance, and for a divine adjustment to be made, at the same time going forward, doing what we know inwardly to be right rather than follow the path of least resistance. Through so doing we find everything working together sweetly and harmoniously.

November 17

In the whole, that which is quite perfect, when it is in its proper place in the whole, becomes imperfect or evil when it is out of its right place in the whole. This is symbolised by the story of Lucifer who left heaven and set up an opposition kingdom, so to speak, of his own. Thus, we see that which is perfectly good when it forms part of the whole becomes disorderly when it leaves the divine order.

November 18

In some way, we benefit by the training which this vast journey in time and space gives. We know that this is the case, because after we have passed through a dark experience, we feel that we are wiser, and know God better, than before the experience; and so, we declare that we would not have missed the experience on any account.

November 19

Suddenly, we realise that our soul is breathing, and that we are developing interior respiration. As we breathe with our lungs, we become conscious of a deeper breathing by our soul taking place at the same time. Unlike yoga breathing, it is not developed by us, but it comes upon us. It descends, so to speak, from heaven, and takes possession of us, so that our physical breathing is regulated and conforms to the pattern and rhythm of the hidden life of God.

November 20

Each requires a Gethsemane experience in order to bring about that change of purpose from self-centredness to God-centredness, which is necessary if ever we are really to know God. We have to be brought to a state of extremity – of complete nothingness – in which we acknowledge that we have come to the end of self, and that there is nothing left but God. It is only in this way that we can become free. The self is our greatest enemy. But we cannot fight it; we cannot destroy it: we can only dissolve it by putting God first.

November 21

All the chastenings of life are due to the fact that we are not in the stream of blessedness. We attract them to ourselves, and bring them into our life, through not living in harmony with the divine. We do not heed the heavenly impulses from within which would fain guide us into the paths of peace and harmony. We still follow the impulses of self, still live in a state of spiritual lethargy, instead of braving the mountain passes of spiritual attainment.

November 22

Owing to the working of a beneficent law – the operation of divine love and wisdom – the effect of our own thinking and acting is that what is brought to us is not punishment, but remedial experience. Thus, it is that one of the secrets of the true art of living is to meet all life's experience with cooperation, and in a flexible and adaptable manner.

November 23

If we hold steadily to the thought that we are immortal, spiritual beings, living in a spiritual universe, governed by spiritual laws, and abide in the consciousness of our sonship, then we are led to act like children of God: to be steadfast, uncomplaining, flexible, and teachable. Not only so – but inward powers are brought into expression, powers which belong to the spiritual self, and not to the material creature. And, also, we are raised above the things which vex and grieve the heart, and above the forces and powers which hold us captive.

November 24

All mystery teachings emphasise the fact that there is a very narrow entrance to the king's chamber, that it is only through humbleness and self-abandonment that the way can be found, symbolised in various ways, and in our Lord's teaching by the camel going through the needle gate, which necessitated the animal kneeling down and being unloaded. We all have to pass this way, for if we do not, we travel along a counterfeit path, which looks like the original but does not lead to life.

November 25

Our Lord comes to us, saying: Be not dismayed. I will make up for all you have lost. I will satisfy the hunger of your soul, the thirst of your spirit and the deep longing of your heart. I will be more to you than anything you have lost. Instead of ephemeral things, I give you that which can never fade away. Instead of the human love which may have failed you, I give you my love which can never fail. I give you myself. Instead of the tinsel of life, I give you the riches of my grace. I will be in you a well of water springing up into everlasting life and joy and satisfaction.

November 26

God gives us His life. He implants it in us. He shares it with us, so that we *"taste and see that the Lord is good."* We taste the immortal sweetness of the life of the spirit. This is not the ordinary life (breath) of animals and physical beings but is the immortal life of the unchanging God.

November 27

We may be overtaken by a great sorrow, loss or trouble, and may be frantic with grief for a time – not on our own account, of course, but on account of another, or others. At such a time we should strive to realise that God is the only doer and that He does all things well. We should not give way to grief and fear about what has happened but should concentrate upon staying our mind upon God instead, endeavouring to realise that the Lord is our light and salvation, and that what He is to us, He is also to our loved ones.

November 28

It is through choosing the difficult path that we find ourselves in a state of freedom: it is through choosing the easy path that we find life increasingly difficult. If we seek the personal happiness of the selfhood, we never find it: if we follow the painful path of duty and high achievement, we find rest to our soul, and joy which transcends mere happiness, even as the mountain towers above the plain.

November 29

It is through being in mental conflict with the disciplinary experience of life that many evils arise. Thus, we have a paradox, which is, that if we accept life's experiences, thus accepting anything that life may bring, we not only rise above fear and apprehension, because we accept that which we have feared, but we also avoid the suffering that conflict and strain, due to opposition, cause. Through experience and through meditation, being helped and instructed by the spirit, we enter into an inner understanding of this great truth.

November 30

"Our Father." That is the perfect attitude. God, first and always; yet God, the great and supreme being of the whole universe of infinity, is our Father. If we maintain this attitude, then we gradually unfold, and in time enter into truth, realising that our true life is lived in God, and that God lives in us. Then we see God everywhere; for God sees only Himself reflected in all things and beings, and so to the extent that God dwells in us do we see God everywhere.

CHAPTER TWELVE

December

December 1

God gives us no guarantee for the future. We can only trust Him. If God were to give us guarantees, then we would be tempted to trust in guarantees instead of in Him. So, we are given no guarantee, that we may trust God only.

We have to step out into the void. Then, if we do this, we find the rock beneath our feet. Nothing before, nothing behind, nothing under our feet, apparently. We have to step out into the unknown, trusting only in Him – the One who can never fail.

December 2

If we feel that all things are possible, or that the impossible is possible, then it really is possible. This feeling comes to us as a result of waiting upon God in the silence. We do not wait upon God in order to arrive at that state of consciousness in which we know and feel that the so-called impossible is possible. No, we wait upon

God to find God, for His own sake, and not for any reward. Then, if our motive is pure and sincere, the feeling of infinite power and adequacy which we experience is one of the things added: it is a gift of divine grace.

December 3

Many of us make the mistake of thinking that if we were somewhere else and our circumstances easier, we could get on better, and that if we were possessed of more capital or were blessed by more brains or greater ability, we could make our life truly successful. And also, in the same way, if we lived in a more spiritual environment, and if we were spiritual geniuses, then we might become seers or saints. But of course, this is quite wrong. We have to start where we are and use what we have.

December 4

Every time that we enter the silence – which, by the way, is the highest form of positive spiritual activity, and not a general negative receptivity which must be avoided – every time that we thus enter the presence of the living God, as children, a certain amount of fashioning takes place. The change is gradual, like the growth of a plant. Indeed, it is so gradual that we seem to be making no progress, at times. But so long as we persevere in our meditations, so long does the work of change and refashioning proceed.

December 5

If we go forward, to do and to dare (instead of trying to live sheltered lives) health and achievement, true success and all that is truly worthwhile come to us. If we go forward, the Lord is with us, the blessing of Jehovah is ours, the blessing which maketh rich and with which He addeth no sorrow. In other words, conflict is avoided, so that the divinely normal life, which is good and perfect, can find expression.

December 6

Neither looking at the past, nor regarding the future, I think only of the present, relying entirely upon Thee, who art the Lord of my life. I live only one day at a time, leaving tomorrow to take care of the things of itself. Doing, through grace, the right thing today, and being faithful in all that I have to do today, enable me to leave the future with Thee. Being led by the spirit in all things, I am guided to do today that which will bring a harvest of blessing in the future. Therefore, I have no anxiety or care. All strain and fear are gently laid aside, and I rest confidently in Thee.

December 7

The reason why many of us are so frustrated and bewildered, so I think, is that we look upon this earth-life as a sort of picnic or outing. Instead of which it is a training and a most valuable opportunity for reaching liberation and final bliss in divine union.

Consequently, we meet with repeated frustrations. This could not be otherwise, for the simple reason that whereas life is trying to lead us one way, we are trying desperately to go in the opposite direction.

December 8

Many are frightened by the idea of surrender. But it is a surrender to love. Is there anything dreadful in that? When we surrender to God; when we let go of the rope of self-effort and self-sufficiency, we fall into the arms of God, who is love to all eternity.

With regard to acceptance, we cannot overcome anything without we first accept it. If we wait for the tide to turn, as it surely will do, then we find ourselves buoyed up by the waves of blessedness; and whereas previously everything ran away from us, now everything flows to us.

December 9

How I long that all seekers should know this: that we do not have to fight our troubles, or those who appear to be the cause of them, but only to find God's inward peace, after which we experience and see blessing upon blessing unfolding in our life and affairs. Verily, if we seek God first, not trying to have our life made easier, then all manner of divine good seeks us and strives to enter our life. We do not seek it: instead, it seeks us.

December 10

Let it be said that the realisation of God's peace cannot be forced: it must come naturally. If we try to force ourselves to feel the peace of God, then we prevent it from coming to us. Whereas, if we dwell in the secret place of the Most High, then what is the greatest of all blessings will come to us, of its own volition, when we least expect it.

It is not the result of much thinking, or of strenuous seeking; neither is it achieved through spiritual exercises. No, it is through becoming quiet in God, and receptive to God.

December 11

We cannot bribe God to give us the Kingdom by giving up this, that, or the other; but when we have surrendered ourselves, and our all, we see clearly that there are things in our life which have to go. There are areas in our life and being, and fortresses in our heart, into which the Lord has never yet been allowed to enter. All barriers have to be taken down and all self-will surrendered, in order that the old, false self may be dethroned, and the Lord within allowed to rule in us without any opposition whatever.

December 12

Thou art unchanging and unfailing. Thou who hast cared for me and who hast loved me, and hast protected and provided for me all these years, will always continue to do so. Yea, Thine everlasting and almighty arms are forever underneath me, and though Heaven and earth were to pass away, they would still support me. Therefore, whatever may befall me, and no matter what may happen to me, love can never fail, and I am still in perfect security in Thy care.

December 13

The cause of disease and poverty is a spiritual one. So also, of course, is the cause of war. We cannot overcome any of these things by fighting them or struggling against them, because behind them are powers of intense potency. We can overcome them only by realising the divine presence which is infinite good, and which is positive, and which is the reality – God. God is the everlasting Yea and Amen. He is the eternal Positive, and all evil is a departure from the real and true.

December 14

Our Father, who art in Heaven, hallowed be Thy name. Thy Kingdom come. Thy will be done in earth as it is in Heaven. Let Thy Kingdom come in this body of mine, and let Thy will of love, light and good be done in it, even as it is in the light body, or the glorious body of the Lord.

December 15

If our main attention is directed towards our own bodily healing, then we actually bypass God, and thus cut ourselves off from our divine centre and source and, as a result, remain in the wilderness.

The real object of our life on this plane is to bring us into a state of divine union or liberation. If therefore we bypass God in our prayers, then we may pray for a certain thing for years without receiving an answer. In the words of St James, we ask and receive not, because we ask amiss.

Yet, if we leave off praying for a certain thing or blessing, then probably the very thing which refused to come to us when we prayed for it, now comes to us.

December 16

When a time of difficulty begins to approach us, instead of repining, or resisting (rebelling) or fearing, or becoming depressed, we should rejoice because so great a blessing is on the way. So instead of praying for help we can praise God for the great blessing that is already coming to us. Instead of concentrating upon the approaching trouble, we can praise and bless the Lord, in whom we live and have our being, and who lives in us, and who fills us with His power.

December 17

It is a fact that if we try to practise the modicum of truth that we know, then greater understanding comes to us; and also, strength and power are given to us, or rather grow up within us, for everything comes from within.

In the course of time, we enter into God-consciousness, so that we think, feel and speak from the divine consciousness.

December 18

We cannot create perfection, for perfection already is. All that we can do is to allow the hidden splendour to appear. More and more do we desire to become a channel through which the divine power and perfection can flow unimpeded. If we realise the truth, and put aside all our own ideas and opinions, so that the self can no longer hinder or distort God's ideas, thus making it possible for them to flow through us without distortion, then the divine perfection will appear. Thus, the world will be changed, and also its peoples.

December 19

A few simple rules:
(1) Follow the teachings of Jesus.
(2) Remember that at all times love is the key to every situation in life, and that God is love to all eternity.
(3) Pray without ceasing. This can be achieved by inwardly thank-

ing God for countless blessings at all times; in course of time, it becomes a subconscious habit.

(4) Learn to relax and allow your breathing to become free.

(5) Keep your mind stayed on God; that is, your highest conception of goodness and perfection, for what you contemplate, that you become.

(6) Forgive to the uttermost those who wrong or injure you in any way. Pray that they may be blest and prospered, and desire it with all the strength of your being.

December 20

You belong to that which is never disturbed or affected by outward events – the inward and eternal, and which, in your true essence, you really are. "For we know that if our earthly house of this tabernacle were dissolved, we have a building of God, an house not made with hands, eternal in the Heavens".

That is your true body, like unto the Lord's glorious resurrection body, clothing the real YOU. Eternal in the Heavens. That is your true state. It is your true state NOW.

December 21

There is no strain or tension in the right use of the imagination. We do not try to relax, we simply let go. There is no strain or effort about that. The power of the imagination is greater than that of the will; therefore, there is no need to use willpower at all. Divine action takes place when we become still and simply contemplate the divine order and perfection.

December 22

Many of us have had moments when all anxiety fell away, and we entered into a state of infinite spaciousness and freedom, and we felt perfectly at home in God. This has been regarded by many as a unique, mystical experience, only vouchsafed to a special and select few. It is a God-given experience for which we cannot be too grateful, but it is, nevertheless, simply a moment of complete relaxation. All at once, it happens, when we least expect it, generally when we are engaged in the humdrum duties of life; in the twinkling of an eye, we pass from time into eternity, from disorder and strain into the divine order and the peace which passeth all (human) understanding.

December 23

A favourite text of mine is: "Unto Him that is able to do exceeding abundantly above all that we ask or think, according to the power that worketh in us". God is able to do great things through us by the power of His Spirit which He has implanted within us. Wonderful things are not done for us, but through us, by the inward power of the indwelling Spirit.

December 24

Mystically speaking, the holy babe is born in us and is then wrapped in numerous wrappings and laid in a manger. This means that it is covered up with ideas of selfhood and separateness, after which it is laid in a manger, which means that it is put into a materialistic environment.

However, in the course of years the materialistic wrappings begin to wear thin, so that some of the light imprisoned begins to shine through. This may continue for years, during which the soul may pass through many experiences, each one of which will wear away the occluding material; until at last the hidden glory bursts through in all its fullness.

December 25

We read in Job of a wonderful thing at the birth of creation; we're told that "the morning stars sang together, and all the sons of God shouted for joy". The sons of God shouted for joy because it was the birth of creation – the beginning of a glorious work of creative life. In the same way, we rejoice in a specially happy way over the birth of that perfect life which was later to blossom into the perfect flower of humanity.

Yet what is known as "Christmas" is something more than a festival. It is also something far more than a celebration of something which happened nearly 2,000 years ago. It is the beginning of a new life. We stand on the brink of a great mystery.

December 26

There takes place the fecundation of the soul by the Holy Ghost, who places within it a seed of the divine Logos. In due course, this seed germinates, after which there begins a process of change. A new self arises – the Christ self. Then commences a struggle by the old selfish self with the new selfless self or Christ. The "child" or new Christ self within the soul grows stronger, while "the self" gradually becomes weaker. Thus, we see a great change taking place in a person, over, perhaps, some years. They are the same, yet quite different, for they no longer care for the things which once they delighted in and love the things which once they disliked.

December 27

Some may wonder why it is that, in spite of their faith, they are never healed, or that, if they are healed, the healing does not prove permanent. The reason is, I believe, that they are still clinging to self. They have not yet "let go of the rope".

It appears to the aspiring soul that something has gone wrong, and that therefore something must be put right. And so frantic prayer is made to God to alter matters. Or in other words, that they may be enabled to continue clinging to the rope. But God says: "Let go of the rope".

December 28

If we meet our Gethsemane experience with resistance and try to wipe it out by the use of metaphysical treatments, then we may do ourselves harm and bring our spiritual unfoldment to a standstill. This is because we are working against the will of God instead of co-operating with it. The object of this great experience of the rope and the abyss is to bring us to the end of "self", so that our will becomes aligned with the perfect will of God. In this alignment lies our highest good.

All the time we strive and struggle against the experiences which cause despair, we are in anguish, but as soon as we let go, we enter into peace. We find ourselves caught in the arms of God.

December 29

If Christ were to reign in the hearts of all people, then the thoughts of all of us would be those of love, justice, goodwill, truth and righteousness. After this everything that is wrong in the world would soon be swept away, for all our actions would be changed. Then Christ would indeed reign on the earth.

December 30

A little girl was asked what she thought the stars might be. She replied that "they must be gimlet holes in the floor of Heaven". A lovely thought, though far from being scientifically correct. In a spiritual sense, however, it is very deeply true; for those who make contact with the world of reality become channels through which divine order and harmony flow.

December 31

I pray that you may be divinely blessed, and upheld, and sustained and supported by the divine Spirit, and upheld in the love of God and kept very near to the heart of God, and that you may know His inward peace, and that it may flow through you like a river. I pray also that you may be so filled with divine love that your life may be a benediction to all whom you meet.

Also by Henry Thomas Hamblin

Thank you for purchasing this book. If you have enjoyed reading it, please consider leaving a review. It takes just a moment, and helps small publishers like us boost the visibility of our books, so that other readers can find our titles. You can scan the relevant QR code for your country of residence, by holding your phone's camera to the code. A prompt will appear, which will take you to the 'leave a review' page. Thank you – your time is much appreciated.

If you are in the UK, use this code

Scan the QR code or type this link into your browser

bit.ly/4eSzCTM

Scan with your phone camera

Hamblin Vision Publishing

THANK YOU!

If you are in the US, use this code

Scan the QR code or type this link into your browser

bit.ly/3UnKsHO

Scan with your phone camera

Hamblin Vision Publishing   THANK YOU!

If you are in Canada, use this code

Scan the QR code or type this link into your browser

bit.ly/4eY8MJV

Scan with your phone camera

Hamblin Vision Publishing   THANK YOU!

If you are in Australia, use this code

Scan the QR code or type this link into your browser

bit.ly/451Lwq6

Scan with your phone camera

Hamblin Vision Publishing   THANK YOU!

Also by Henry Thomas Hamblin

The Stillness of the Infinite

18 Meditations to Deepen Spiritual Awareness through the Progressive Reflective Meditation Method

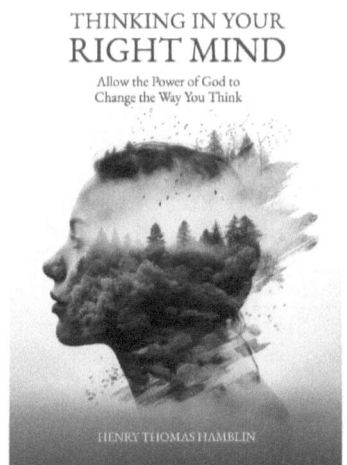

Thinking in Your Right Mind

Allow the Power of God to Change the Way You Think

Within You is the Power

The Inner Secret to Health, Happiness, Success and Abundance

The Secrets of Your Divine Powers

Reconnect with your Spiritual Self to Overcome Obstacles, Heal Your Life and Achieve True Success

The Spiritual Path to True Success

The Practical Mystic's Guide to Living Sucessfully

The Message of a Flower

The Divine Wisdom in Nature

The Worry Antidote

The Practical Mystic's Guide to Living Fearlessly

God the Source of Good

The Practical Mystic's Guide to Living Fearlessly

The Power of Thought

How to unlock the power of your mind to create a life of health, success and prosperity

Powerful Prayers and Psalm 23

The Practical Mystic's guide to three Christian Prayers: The Lord is My Shepherd, The Lord's Prayer and Bless the Lord, O My Soul

HENRY THOMAS HAMBLIN

The titles below are available from our website www.thehamblinvision.org.uk

The Way of the Practical Mystic

My Search for Truth

The Story of my Life

Life Without Strain

Divine Adjustment

The Open Door

Life of the Spirit

His Wisdom Guiding

The Hamblin Book of Daily Readings

God Our Centre and Source

God's Sustaining Grace

www.ingramcontent.com/pod-product-compliance
Lightning Source LLC
Chambersburg PA
CBHW030336010526
44119CB00047B/512